T0247267

MY LIFE

TERRY DAVIES

Copyright © 2024 by Terry Davies

All rights reserved.

No portion of this book may be reproduced in any form without written permission
from the publisher or author, except as permitted by U.S. copyright law.

Print ISBN: 979-8-35097-587-1
eBook ISBN: 979-8-35097-588-8

Printed in the United States of America

***

SOCIAL MEDIA LINKS

Facebook: https://www.facebook.com/terry.davies
Instagram: https://www.instagram.com/tezdaviestad/

DEDICATION

To Anne, who has been my anchor and inspiration

To Nick, whose laughter fills my heart with joy

To Mum and Dad, whose love and nurturing made everything possible.

Thank you for being the pillars of my life's story.

TABLE OF CONTENTS

Dedication   v

Foreword   1

Prologue   3

Chapter 1: Openshaw and Old Trafford   6

Chapter 2: Compassion and Confrontation   12

Chapter 3: Becoming My Own Man   18

Chapter 4: What's the Buzz   23

Chapter 5: Walkabout   28

Chapter 6: What Uncle Harry Taught Me   32

Chapter 7: The Emancipation of Strawberry Pye   36

Chapter 8: A Three-Piece Band   40

Chapter 9: Frontmen and Sidemen   44

Chapter 10: The Strange Pull   48

Chapter 11: The Girl at the Airport   51

Chapter 12: Where's Your Ball?   55

Chapter 13: Lonely Together   61

Chapter 14: California Dreamin'   66

Chapter 15: The Cresting Wave   70

Chapter 16: Looking Forward   74

Chapter 17: Stateside   79

Chapter 18: Communicate   83

Chapter 19: Lion Tamers   89

Chapter 20: Five Thousand Miles   95

Chapter 21: Devastation   98

Chapter 22: Onward and Upward   103

Chapter 23: The Opportunity of a Lifetime   107

Chapter 24: Fazakerley and Skelmersdale   112

Chapter 25: Melting in the Dark   116

Chapter 26: Gigs and Games   120

Chapter 27: Welcome, Nick   124

Chapter 28: My Little Miracle   128

Chapter 29: Fool Me Once   134

Chapter 30: Bad Ideas and Bold Visions   138

Chapter 31: Back in the USA   145

Chapter 32: Just Like Old Times   149

Chapter 33: Pie in the SKYE   153

Chapter 34: The Grand Opening   157

Chapter 35: Having the Time of Your Life   161

Chapter 36: An Unlikely Idol   166

Chapter 37: Turning Point   170

Chapter 38: Songs at Sea   174

Chapter 39: Nature's Wrath   178

Chapter 40: Fathoms Below   182

Chapter 41: An Unexpected Acquisition   186

Chapter 42: City of Gold   189

Chapter 43: Under the Knife   194

Chapter 44: Unbalanced Scales   198

Chapter 45: Nick and Julia   203

Chapter 46: Polar Opposites   208

Chapter 47: Our Happily Ever After   211

Chapter 48: Lucky   217

Chapter 49: Full Circle   223

Chapter 50: A Miracle Revisited   228

Epilogue: It's better to forgive...   234

FOREWORD

By Nick Davies

Reading the true story of your hero's upbringing and learning about how the years of successes, failures, triumphs, mistakes, battles, struggles, trials, and victories molded him into the person you've chosen to idolize is a true gift that is only made more poignant when that hero also happens to be your father. I met my Dad when he already had thirty-four years of stories and life experience under his belt. Through the thirty years that I've been lucky enough to be his son, I've seen my father at his lowest of lows (managing a failing restaurant during the recession), just as I've seen him at his highest of highs (building a multi-million dollar company from the ground up). I've seen him turn the tables of his own life and meticulously create and compose his own destiny and success. Some people will fall into a deep ditch and accept their fate. They will use the limited resources around them to create shelter in an attempt to get comfortable at the bottom. Some people will fall into a deep ditch and use those same resources to build a ladder back to the top. I'm beyond proud to say that my Dad is the type of person who will build his ladder and then subsequently offer it to the people who still find themselves stuck at the bottom of their ditch. Being a CEO of an international company is no easy task, and I'd be lying if I said that I hadn't seen my Dad make his fair share of enemies along the way. Despite that unavoidable truth, my father's constant lifelong commitment and belief in positivity, generosity, and selflessness has resulted in a hundred times as many friends. Those friends, who I have no doubt are currently reading this and eagerly awaiting the story ahead, are all part of my father's incredible journey and have been, in my Dad's words, instrumental in his growth through the years. In return, my Dad tries his best to provide as many opportunities to as many people as he can, all while keeping his family his number one priority, with Manchester United Football Club being a close second. Ask almost anyone who knows me, and they will say that I get my sense of humor, zest for life, spontaneity, generosity, positivity, creativity, and musical talent from my Dad. I say "almost" because my mom insists I get it from her; a statement with which I, along with my Dad, would have trouble disagreeing.

I know how lucky I am to have the relationship with my father that I do. I laugh with him. I cry with him. We make fun of each other. We bond over our mutual obsessions with Billy Joel and Back to the Future. We celebrate each other through our successes and inspire each other through our failures. I live the most amazing life with him. I very nearly died with him. I've quite literally traveled the world with him. I've performed music with him on a thousand stages to a thousand audiences and my only wish after every show is that there will be a thousand more. People often ask me if I'm going to walk in my father's footsteps. The truth is, I first need to step into his shoes and believe me when I say, they are extremely big shoes to fill. All I know is that most of the opportunities that I have been dealt in my life thus far would have never happened if it weren't for my Dad and though it sometimes seems impossible to me, I only hope that he's as proud of me as I am of him.

Terry Davies is a dreamer.

Terry Davies is a warrior.

Terry Davies is my best friend.

Terry Davies is my father, and this is his story.

PROLOGUE

As I sit down to pen the prologue to my autobiography, I am filled with a sense of gratitude and accomplishment. It's imperative, I think, that those two feelings always go hand-in-hand--too many highly accomplished people lose sight of how they got to where they are. Ingratitude is an ugly thing, never uglier than when it's being showcased by someone who's "made it." I'll tell you a little secret: nobody makes it all by themselves.

This book chronicles my journey from humble beginnings in Manchester, England, to becoming a successful musician, performer, and entrepreneur in the USA and beyond. Through these pages, I hope to share with you the highs and lows of my life, the challenges I've faced, and the lessons I've learned. It's a tall order, but I like to imagine that I'm up to it. My goal, simply put, is to give you a sense of what it's been like to be me, for the last sixty-odd years. I won't lie to you, mine hasn't always been an enviable position to be in. But complaints are, at this moment, the furthest thing from my mind.

Why is the story of my life worth telling? In short, because if my life had happened to anybody else, there are parts of it that I would frankly have a hard time believing. I've been so incredibly fortunate. For half a century now I've been a believer in the power of grit, hard work and dedication, and I'd like to say I have them to thank for my success. But I also believe that luck plays a big part in our lives--a far bigger part than many self-made men are prepared to admit to themselves. And boy, have I been lucky. It was once leveled at me that the only reason I have had any success at all was all down to being lucky. Aaah – the bliss of ignorance driven by anger and jealousy...but we'll get into that a little later in the book. Throughout this book, you will see the occasional quote that has inspired me, one way or another. One of my favorites is by Mark Twain ~ "*It ain't what you don't know that gets you into trouble. It's what you know for sure that just ain't so*".... so true!

I don't claim to be especially wise, but I have seen a lot of what the world has to offer, and I've picked up a thing or two, here and there, in my travels. Some combination of luck, talent and drive has carried me along, every step of the way, from cramped British tenements to the sun-drenched coasts of Spain, from hole-in-the-wall bars to sprawling festival stages. An itinerant musician acquires new stories and soaks up new experiences the same way he learns new songs. I've been adding all sorts of crazy sights and sounds to my personal repertoire ever since I was a wide-eyed, cash-strapped teenager in the mid-1970s. Since then, it's been my privilege to perform for audiences around the world, culminating in the ultimate thrill: sharing the spotlight with my amazing son, Nick. How he came to be, and how he upended my life, is one tale that I cannot wait to tell you. All in due time.

The story of my musical career cannot be told in isolation, you see. At every stage of the journey we're about to go on, my life has influenced my art, and my art has changed the trajectory of my life. I've acted recklessly, and made mistakes, and scrambled madly through entire decades without any sort of safety net under me. Still, I can't shake the feeling, looking back over it all, that I ultimately wound up exactly where I was meant to be--the place where I am at my happiest.

I have my regrets--who doesn't?--but perspective is everything. There was a period in my life when playing music for a living seemed like an impossible dream, and another period when having a child likewise seemed unattainable. That I am now able to perform with my son Nick on a nightly basis is nothing short of miraculous. The job I have tasked myself with in writing this book, is to explain to you how it was that this improbable miracle was achieved.

I've been playing music since I was a small boy. To say that it has been a lifelong companion would be an understatement. It is closer to an incorporeal part of my body, a phantom appendage or vital organ of some kind. It will never show up on an x-ray, but it is as essential to my survival as my heart or lungs. It is both an instrument of perception and a means of expression--it is an extra pair of eyes with which I see, as well as an extra mouth through which I speak. It has clung to me like an invisible second shadow aboard boats and buses and in countless cheap hotel rooms. It has saved my life on more than one occasion, and it has also put me in harm's way. There are myriad points in the story you're about to read at which my life might have ended. Any one of those untimely endings would have erased this book from existence.

Read on, and you'll hear all about how I thought I was going to drown at sea in my twenties and how I almost died on a highway last year. Maybe I'm writing this book now and getting all these scattered thoughts on paper so that they'll have a shot at outliving me. Life is fragile and fleeting. If I should happen to glance up one day and see a tidal wave or a pair of headlights bearing down on me, at least I'll know I got all these stories out of my system. Or maybe my motivation isn't quite so morbid as that––maybe all I really want to do, when all is said and done, is give thanks and answer a deceptively simple question for myself. How did I find my way from a muddy side street in Openshaw to a skyscraper in Dubai? The shortest, truest answer that I can muster up is that I didn't do it alone. I think, on balance, that I've lived a rather incredible life––but it's the people in it who have made it so incredible. Everything else is just the frosting on the proverbial cake.

The path that I've taken through life has been shaped by the values of loyalty, fairness, and dedication to family that I hold dear. I could not begin to name all the people I have known who were responsible for imparting those values to me, and who therefore deserve credit for what I've become––credit for this very book. You will find their names scribbled into every last chapter of it. This modest prologue you're reading now could not possibly hope to contain them all. Having said that, I've already name-dropped Nick––and how could I not?––so it's only fair that I single out one other person as well before I get down to business and kick off this show.

Anne––I love you. This book is yours as much as it's mine. It is, after all, the story of my life––and my life is yours.

CHAPTER 1:
OPENSHAW AND OLD TRAFFORD

Manchester is the belly and guts of the nation
—George Orwell

* * *

The life of a musician is an endless chain of challenges. There's no shortage of obstacles to overcome and disasters to circumvent. The upside of the lifestyle, in theory, is that you meet loads and loads of other musicians. Everyone who's ever picked up an instrument or a microphone and stepped onstage, everyone who's ever hustled and scrounged and gone hungry for the chance to make music, will understand what you're up against without ever having to be told. There's a natural camaraderie among people who make a living playing music––most of the time. Every now and then you cross paths with a fellow musician who is, himself, a challenge, an obstacle, and a disaster. People like that are the one part of the struggle of musicianship that I have the hardest time tolerating.

I was only sixteen or so when I first found myself backed into a corner by an individual like the one I've just described. I had just joined up with a band called The Fontaines, and I was keen to not embarrass myself or make my bandmates second-guess having brought me on board. When you're young and starting out, those ought to be your two biggest concerns. I would have liked to have been able to just focus on the music and the performance. Jim Fontaine, the band's frontman, founder, and resident petty tyrant, made that impossible. He made himself the number one concern of everyone in his orbit, and I suspect that's how he liked it.

By the time my second gig with The Fontaines rolled around, I was already tired of putting up with Jim's moodiness and drunken tirades. I was sick of being shouted at, mainly. But even the quieter moments (or the moments when his rage was being directed at someone else) were hard to bear. You were always on guard around Jim Fontaine, always on eggshells. You had to swallow your pride and defer to him. If you couldn't manage that, then it was safest to try and just stay out of his way.

That was what I had been trying to do. But as we had a show to put on that evening, it was easier said than done. You couldn't just disappear. You had to be present and play the music. That's what it was all supposed to be about.

My father, Andy Davies, was a musician, and he saw to it that music was a big part of my upbringing. His love for music rubbed off on me from the start. I remember him taking me with him to gigs at a very early age, and the feeling of joy and excitement I got from hearing him play, and from seeing the reactions he got from the crowd. I can still remember thinking, *That's what I want to do when I grow up!* It was an incredibly pure feeling, one that I know my father also felt deeply. Watching Jim Fontaine spew venom at everyone around him like a tinpot dictator was so offensive to me, in part, because it was like seeing him trample upon and tarnish that sense of purity. The starry-eyed wonder that I felt as a child watching my Dad perform had no place in Jim's band. And yet my Dad himself had played in The Fontaines before I ever had and in fact, I directly replaced him in the band when I was just 17. How had the two of them ever managed to put on shows together? The dissonance there didn't sit right with me, and I didn't understand it. That was the mystery I was trying to wrap my head around, the night that Jim Fontaine pushed me too far, and I learned, for the first time, what sort of man I was going to become.

* * *

I was born in Ancoats Hospital on February 28th, 1959, and grew up on Randolph Street in Openshaw, Manchester. One of my earliest memories is of looking out my bedroom window and seeing a man on horseback moving slowly down Randolph Street. He was wielding a strange device, one that I had never seen before, one that he was using to extinguish the gas lamps as he trotted along. It was a surreal and mysterious sight, and it remains a special memory. I'm sure I didn't think to question it at the time (children have a way of taking strange sights in stride), but looking back on it now, it sounds rather incongruous--almost anachronistic. It's as though that horseman came clopping out of some bygone era just to pay me a visit and give me something worth remembering. I've done a bit of Googling, and from what I can tell, Manchester started ditching gas lamps in favor of electric ones in the early 1960s, which means that I could not have been more than a couple of years old when this event occurred. Like everyone else, I have a handful of hazy, vague impressions of my early childhood, but by their very nature, they're not easy to pin down. Glimpsing that man and his horse and his lamp snuffer is the oldest memory that I can roughly put a date to, and it's one that I treasure.

My childhood was spent running up and down cobbled streets, playing with friends, and discovering my love for two things above all else: football and music. These two passions would come to shape my life in ways I never could have imagined.

Manchester in the 1960s was a haven for lovers of football and music, and a hub of pop culture.

We had two of the most iconic football clubs of the era--Manchester United and Manchester City--drawing attention and support from around the world. Fans flocked to matches between the two clubs, making Old Trafford and Maine Road some of the hottest tickets in town. The clubs have been rivals ever since they were founded in 1894, but the rivalry has only grown more intense over the years. I got swept up in it as a small boy. There was no avoiding it. Football was a fact of life.

In addition to its football offerings, Manchester was a major player in the pop music scene. The city was home to major acts like The Bee Gees, The Hollies, and Herman's Hermits, all of which were influential bands during the 1960s and all of which continue to be enjoyed by fans today. The fashion and art scenes in Manchester also thrived during that period. The same pubs, clubs, and music venues that hosted the famous bands also showcased emerging fashion designers and local artwork. As a result, Manchester became known internationally as a vibrant, creative city.

It was stimulating, as a child, to feel that you were growing up in the middle of all that cultural commotion, even if some of its finer points were lost on you. I was obsessed with the worlds of football and music and relatively disinterested in the worlds of fashion and the arts, as you can imagine.

1960's Openshaw

Nevertheless, I got the sense that each of these separate worlds was stronger, somehow, for its proximity to the others. They propped each other up, you might say. The general feeling, all through my adolescence, was that exciting things were happening in Manchester. The city had something for everyone.

∗ ∗ ∗

"They'll forget all the rubbish when I've gone, and they'll remember the football. If only one person thinks I'm the best player in the world, that's good enough for me"
~ George Best

From a young age, football owned my eyes, just as music owned my ears. I harbored a dream of becoming a footballer (which somehow, in my youthful imagination, never came into conflict with my desire to play music when I got older). Growing up in Manchester, it was impossible not to be a fan of the local team, Manchester United. I idolized players like Bobby Charlton and Denis Law, and I spent countless hours kicking a ball around with my friends, practicing my skills, and dreaming of becoming the next George Best. In retrospect, I should add, I had no chance…I was useless at football! Nevertheless, I wouldn't trade those childhood football games and the childlike ambitions that came with them for anything. For several years the cobbled streets of Openshaw, just two miles from Manchester City Center, were my playground, my pitch, and my favorite place in the world.

The day that I became enraptured by football, the day that my love for the sport and for United truly took hold, was December 16th, 1967. That was the day my Dad took me to Old Trafford for the first time. We won 3-1 that day, and I won't ever forget the feeling of euphoria and pride that came over me as I watched my early heroes take to the pitch. Their victory was our victory. It felt like there was really nothing separating the players on the field from me and my Dad celebrating on the sidelines. That is a moment that will stay with me forever.

For me, football was more than just a sport. It was a way of connecting with my father, who shared my love for the game. Going to matches together became a ritual for us, a bond that could never be broken. I will always be grateful for my memories of the joy and togetherness that I felt every time we watched Manchester United play.

Even though my dreams of becoming a professional footballer didn't come to fruition (because, again, I was crap at football), my love for the game has never waned. And whenever I think back to those early days, watching my heroes play at

Old Trafford, I am reminded of the deep connection that I shared with my father until the day he died and the memories that we created together.

He was not a perfect man, my father, and it would be fair to say that he passed a few of his imperfections down to me. We can't control what parts of our parents' personalities we wind up with through some combination of nature and nurture. Half of the struggle of growing into adulthood, I think, is consciously deciding which aspects of your parents you want to keep and which ones you want to drop. There are pieces of my Dad that I have had to discard as I've matured in order to get what I wanted out of life. This discarding process began, I see now, the night that I was set to play my second gig with The Fontaines. For you to appreciate the importance of what happened that fateful night, however, I must first tell you a bit more about my upbringing, my parents, and the lessons they taught me--both intentionally and unintentionally.

I want to stress, in this moment, that there are aspects of my father that I would never willingly part with. These are pieces that I have permanently incorporated into my sense of who I am. Thinking back on that day toward the end of 1967 when he took me to Old Trafford, and we cheered together for United, has reminded me of all of them.

CHAPTER 2:
COMPASSION AND CONFRONTATION

A parent's love is whole no matter how many times divided
—Robert Brault

* * *

Given that I eventually grew into a professional musician, it's easy to look back and see all the little ways in which I was nudged in that direction as a youngster. I have to remind myself as I write this, that my path through life was anything but obvious to me back then. You're exposed to so many new ideas and experiences at that age that it's hard not to feel like you're exploding with potential and that you could wind up practically anywhere if you put your mind to it (that's why I don't give myself a hard time for thinking that I had what it took to play for Manchester United). My education played a significant role in all of this, of course. Attending St. Vincent's Roman Catholic Primary School in Openshaw was a big part of my early years. I have fond memories of my time there, and there are still some school friends from the early 1960s that I'm still in touch with on Facebook.

However, it was outside of school that I truly came alive. Not just in the streets where I ran and played with my friends, but also at home, where my parents were quick to cultivate my musical potential. I've already talked at length about my father but I also cannot say enough kind things about my mother, Pauline. That woman was a force of nature. I can see that now, as a parent, in a way that I could not when I was younger. She was a dedicated mother of eight children, and her love for us was boundless. I believe that even if there had been twice as many of us, she would have still found a way to make each of us feel cherished and understood. As the eldest child, I was privy to her fierce love and unwavering loyalty, and I saw those traits carry on (and, in many ways, get stronger) through each and every one of my siblings. In her eyes, her kids could do no wrong. But to an unbiased observer, reality told quite a different story!

Growing up, my siblings and I tested our mother's patience time and time again (some of us much more than others). I have 4 brothers and 3 sisters - Susan, David, Wendy, Andrew, Peter, Wesley and Jamie-Lee.

We were always pushing boundaries and getting into trouble. But no matter what we did, our Mum never gave up on any of us. Even when we made mistakes or let her down, her love for us never wavered. If her patience had a limit, the eight of us never found it, even with our combined powers and our shared gift for mischief.

As I got older, I began to appreciate just how much my mother sacrificed for her children. She became pregnant with me when she was only seventeen. She gave up her own dreams and aspirations to raise us, and she did so with an unswerving sense of purpose and dedication. Her love for us was the glue that held our family together, and we were all better for it. Had my brothers and sisters and I never come along, her life would have been wholly different. I don't believe she had any regrets, however. And certainly, none of us could have asked for a better mother. There's so much more that I could say about my relationship with my Mum, and it would never be enough.

* * *

My mother was just 17 when I came into this world, yet she embraced motherhood with a devotion that shaped my entire life.

Until her passing in 2013, she showered me with unwavering love and care. She had a gift for using quotes, often misquoting them like her famous "Patience is a virtued!" Her days at McConachie's biscuit factory in Hadfield, packaging chocolate biscuits, sparked my lifelong love for Penguin biscuits. I fondly remember her bringing home boxes of broken ones, which became my cherished treats.

Later in life, when we were at Skye, Jack Jones, one of my Mother's favorite singers, was performing there for four days, culminating with a show on Mother's Day. Needless to say, my Mum was giddy about this. I reserved a table for her very close to the stage. Jack Jones was her idol when she was in her twenties, and here she was, getting ready to watch him sing at her son's venue. She would tell anyone the story who would listen.

When Mother's Day arrived, and it was showtime, she found her way to her VIP table and sat there with the 30-year-old vinyl record she had brought with her to get signed. Just before the show, I chatted with Jack and told him it was also My Mum's birthday in addition to it being Mother's Day. He was preparing for the show - and Jack was always meticulous at this time - so he appeared a little dismissive when I told him. Nothing could have been further from the truth. Literally seconds before he was about to start, he said to me, "Terry, what is your Mum's name?" I told him, "Pauline", and thought nothing of it. Now Jack always began his show at Skye by entering from the back of the room, walking through the audience and singing his first song, "I Am A Singer". It was an incredible opening to a show. On this night, it went a little differently. The band began playing the first song ~ "Ladies and Gentlemen - The One and Only - Mr Jack Jones!" Jack began walking through the audience, shaking a few hands, but he wasn't singing. The band continued to play the introduction over and over again. Jack got to the middle of the audience and asked over the microphone, "Where's Pauline? Where's Pauline?" Of course, my Mum, not being the slightest bit shy, stood up, waved, and shouted, "I'm here!" Jack walked over to my Mum's table and said, "Hi ~ I'm Jack." He sat down next to her and sang the entire first song directly to her. I'm not sure she heard any of it, as she was crying through the whole song. Tears streamed down her face, and mine too, in that unforgettable moment. After the first song, the show continued as normal—it was a fantastic show, but I will only ever remember those three minutes when he made my Mum's dreams come true. Mum only lived a couple more years after this night before she passed away, but I am certain that if you take memories to your grave, this memory went with her for eternity.

* * *

Despite the challenges of raising a family on a limited income, my parents always encouraged my passions and supported my dreams. Looking back, I realize how lucky I was to have such a loving and supportive family. That is something that has carried with me throughout my life, and something I've always tried to bear in mind when raising my own son.

In most respects, my parents were a terrific match. That was my sense of things as a child, anyway, which means they must have been doing something right. My Dad was a gentle and kind man who loved his wife and kids. He was a naturally talented musician with a passion for playing the organ and piano that was infectious.

But as much as I loved my Dad, there was no denying the fact that he had a side to his personality that haunted me for years. One that I imagine must have caused problems in his marriage, even if I could not see them when I was young. He was terribly afraid of confrontation (something that I inherited) and would go to great lengths to avoid any kind of conflict. This made him an easy target for bullies and abusers. In my experience, people like that become very adept at sniffing out weaknesses in others and exploiting them. My Dad fell prey to that sort of exploitation more than I care to recount. But his unwillingness to defend himself never pained me more during my adolescence than when I saw the bullying and abuse that he put up with during his time stint in The Fontaines.

Jim Fontaine was a notorious womanizer and heavy drinker who treated people poorly. It's apparent to me now that he was an alcoholic, but even recognizing that doesn't make it any easier for me to sympathize with him. I watched as he pushed my Dad around and belittled him, and I felt helpless to do anything about it. It was a difficult thing to witness, especially because my Dad was such a goodhearted person who didn't deserve to be treated that way.

Even after my Dad left The Fontaines, his fear of confrontation came back to haunt him again and again, perhaps never more so than when my parents got divorced. He struggled to assert his needs and stand up for himself, which made the process even more difficult. It was a sad realization for me, made sadder by the fact that his meekness was something that I recognized in myself. Growing up, I saw over and over how my Dad's fear of confrontation held him back, and I knew that I didn't want to fall into that same trap.

After my father got out from under Jim Fontaine's thumb, he went on to play organ in the clubs of the northwest of England, including The Willows in Salford, Manchester (Salford Rugby Club). It always made me happy seeing him perform, particularly when he wasn't being hounded by the likes of Jim Fontaine, and was able to fully enjoy himself without fear of being made to feel inferior. It hurt me, as a kid, seeing him being mistreated--every boy wants to believe that his Dad is a strong, tough figure--but as I age, I find myself questioning how much it must have hurt him, knowing that his own son was bearing witness to that mistreatment. I wonder if he recognized what sort of example he was setting for me or if he hoped that I would take a different tack when I started running into intimidating and disagreeable people in my own life, people who would try to mock, control, or walk all over me.

Ultimately, I'm happy (not to mention lucky) to have had the father I had. A caring, creative, sensitive man with a timid disposition makes for a better caretaker, I would say, than a man with an iron will but no other positive qualities. His timidity did not make me love him any less. If anything, the opposite was the case--whenever I saw him bend the knee to someone who wasn't half the man that he was, the anger and hurt that I felt was proof of how much I loved him. There are no perfect parents. Besides, aren't we all supposed to improve upon our fathers and mothers? I have no doubt that my own son will exceed me in countless ways over the coming years. A parent's greatest joy, it seems to me, is watching that process take place and feeling yourself being outstripped by this wonderful person that you raised. I think a lot of young men in my position would have come to harbor bitter feelings about their father to resent his weakness. But I'm proud to say that I've always reserved the lion's share of my bitterness and resentment for the bullies and abusers of the world--for men like Jim Fontaine. Shortly after he recruited me into his band, he discovered that for himself.

CHAPTER 3:
BECOMING MY OWN MAN

The man who makes no mistakes does not usually make anything
—Edward Phelps

* * *

In 1969, when I was ten years old, my family moved to the overspill estate of Gamesley near Glossop in Derbyshire. This was a massive shakeup in my young life and a huge change of scenery from my previous home in Openshaw. With the resourcefulness of youth, however, I quickly adapted to my new surroundings. I attended St. Margaret's school for a couple of years, and I can vividly recall walking to school and taking in the sights and sounds of the countryside for the first time.

The house in Gamesley

The grassy hills and leafy trees were such a contrast to the urban landscape that I had previously called home. Just like that, my eyes were opened to the beauty of the natural world. During this time, I made some good friends, including Nigel Currie, Sheila Sidebottom, Cathy Sayer and Sharon Pounder (apologies to the dozens of schoolfriends I left out). We spent our days exploring the woods and fields, playing music and sports, and dreaming about our futures. Little did we know that some of these friendships would last a lifetime.

Two years later, in 1971, I began attending St. Philip Howard School (or Blessed Philip Howard, as it was called at the time). It was there that I joined the brass band and first picked up the euphonium. I loved that instrument from the moment I got my hands on it and held its mouthpiece to my lips. Thanks to some combination of love and ability (I hesitate to say which deserves more of the credit), I rapidly became proficient on it. I played with the legendary Tintwhistle Brass Band for a while, honing my skills and building my confidence. Along with the euphonium, I continued to play the piano, which had been a passion of mine since I was a child.

My time at St. Philip Howard was a very positive period in my life, and I will always look back on those years with fondness and gratitude. Two of the biggest influences on me back then were a band teacher named John Golland and my music teacher, Terry Walsh. Mr Walsh was the first teacher who showed me that it was OK to love music and have fun with it.

Despite knowing Mr. Golland for far less time (I think he was only with us at St. Philip Howard for a couple of years), I'm tempted to say that he was the more influential of the two. I remember immediately being struck by how different he was from other teachers. He went against the grain and believed deeply in his own way of doing things. He was the only teacher who encouraged me to keep trying my hand at unfamiliar instruments, and his support helped me to not be afraid to try new things musically. When I first met Mr. Golland, I was a shy, introverted student who had always loved music but had never really pursued it seriously.

Mr. Golland saw something in me that I didn't see in myself. He recognized my potential and encouraged me to explore different styles of music and not be afraid to experiment. Under his guidance, I began to play around with the piano as well as other instruments, and in no time at all I discovered a passion for music that I had never known before. His support and encouragement gave me the confidence to push myself creatively and take risks in my musical pursuits.

Looking back, I realize that his influence went far beyond just the realm of music. Mr. Golland was instrumental in developing my confidence and self-assurance, qualities that I needed to succeed in all aspects of my life. He was a true inspiration, and I will always be thankful for the impact that he had on my life.

Armed with a newfound sense of my own musical potential, I began to listen to the popular music of the day more avidly and appreciate it in a deeper way. During my preteen and teenage years, I couldn't get enough of the larger-than-life music of bands like Slade and Wizzard, as well as artists like Stevie Wonder and The Stylistics. My favorite act by far, however, back then and throughout the rest of my life, was Gilbert O'Sullivan. He was quite unlike the rest of the louder, flashier rock stars I gravitated towards, but his songs spoke to me in a way that nothing else did, and I found myself listening to his albums on repeat for hours on end. But he was the exception to the rule. For me, the glam rock era of the 1970s will forever be epitomized by Slade and Wizzard. Both groups were known for their outrageous costumes, catchy hooks, and electrifying live performances, and thanks to this skill and exuberance both groups were at the forefront of the decade's signature musical genre.

Slade was my first love, musically speaking. With their iconic chants of "Cum on Feel the Noize" and "Mama Weer All Crazee Now," they were undoubtedly a force to be reckoned with. Their music was hard-hitting, with driving guitar riffs and pounding drums that never failed to get audiences on their feet and dancing. But it was their natural talent for writing catchy sing-along choruses that made them so successful. *Slade in Flame* was a lousy movie––but I love it anyway!

Wizzard, on the other hand, had a more eclectic sound. Led by the flamboyant Roy Wood, the band fused rock and roll with elements of classical music, creating a unique style that was both grandiose and playful. In many ways, they were similar to ELO. For my money, "See My Baby Jive" is one of the greatest pop songs ever written.

What Slade and Wizzard had in common, in my view, was their ability to capture the spirit of the times. Their music was simultaneously rebellious and fun. Throwing on a Slade or Wizzard album afforded people a temporary escape from the drudgery of everyday life. Both bands were unabashedly loud and proud, inspiring a generation of fans (of which I was one) to embrace their individuality and not make any apologies for it. It's not just nostalgia that keeps me coming back to their old records––some of those tunes are indestructible! But the memories they stir up for me have also made this writing process much easier. I think the highest compliment that you can pay any musical act is that their work perfectly evokes the time in which it was made, while at the same time achieving a timeless quality.

My affinity for rock and roll, and my desire to play it to the best of my ability, meant that I could not refuse the offer to join The Fontaines when my Dad was leaving the band, despite knowing what sort of person Jim Fontaine was. True to form, he immediately began browbeating and abusing me the same way that he had browbeaten and abused my father. It was as though, from his point of view, I had slotted neatly into the hole my Dad had left behind when he quit the band, and so the only thing to do was to treat us identically. Then again, he behaved that way toward everyone in his life. In his eyes, we were all replaceable. He was a bully through and through. Too many people were content to keep their mouths shut and their heads down when he drunkenly lashed out at whoever happened to be within shouting distance. I decided, after only two gigs, that I wasn't going to be one of them. It was not a calculated decision.

To be honest, I don't even remember what it was that set me off. I had simply had enough. It wasn't just his misbehavior that I couldn't tolerate––it was the path of least resistance that I saw laid out before me if I didn't do something, a path that I was terrified of getting stuck on. And so, I strayed from it as quickly and decisively as I could. I told Jim Fontaine, in no uncertain terms, to fuck off. And with that, I stormed out. As I said, this was not premeditated. It came out of a deep-seated, instinctual urge to avoid the senseless abuse that I'd seen my father quietly endure for so many years. I had a temper at that age, and that, combined with my feelings of self-worth, made it unthinkable for me to remain in The Fontaines for one minute longer. So, I left. And I made sure to permanently burn the bridge when I did so.

Telling Jim Fontaine to fuck off was cathartic in the moment, of course, but looking back, I realize that it gave me far more than a fleeting sense of satisfaction. It was a defining moment in my life. From that point on, I was better able to recognize my own fear of confrontation; after that blowup, I knew that I had the strength to overcome it if I just dug deep enough.

My Dad's inability to engage in conflict, even when it would have been in his best interest, was a difficult thing to witness. But witnessing it taught me a valuable lesson about standing up for myself and asserting my needs. That is something I carry with me to this very day. My Dad had compassion for everything and everyone and, thankfully, genetics kicked in and gave me that aspect of his personality as well. It's a great balance.

My father's legacy lives on in me through his love of music and his gentle spirit, but also through the lessons I learned about the importance of never backing down and recognizing when you're not being treated fairly. The music industry is awash in giant egos, and Jim Fontaine was a small fish indeed, compared to some of the sharks that are out there. If you've set your sights on being a musician, do bear in mind that nobody deserves to be dehumanized, badgered, or ridiculed. The moment you find yourself on the receiving end of that kind of abuse, plant your feet and push back.

That's my advice.

The sooner you take that lesson to heart, the happier you'll be.

CHAPTER 4:
WHAT'S THE BUZZ

Growing old is mandatory, but growing up is optional
—Walt Disney

* * *

After finishing school, I found myself at a bit of a crossroads. Like a lot of young people fresh out of secondary school, I wasn't quite sure what I wanted to do with my life. Then, one day, I made a spur-of-the-moment decision that would change my life forever, and in some unforeseen ways. I decided to join the RAF. It wasn't a decision that I had thought through carefully, to be honest. I had spent some time in the air cadets with Nigel Currie when we were younger, and he was joining the Air Force, so I just followed suit. It was probably one of the few times I have followed anyone.

Nigel and I were good friends, but I was equally close with a few of my other schoolmates. It's hard to say just why I followed in his footsteps the way I did. I felt rather directionless at that time, and I suppose there must have been a part of me that was desperate for some kind of structured, easily understood plan to cling to. The appeal of enlisting, for me (to the extent that I thought about it all) was that doing so would eliminate uncertainty from my life. When you're in the Air Force, or any branch of the armed forces, your days are highly regimented, and your decisions are mostly made for you by your superiors. This can be comforting, in a way, for an indecisive young man unsure of his life goals--but as I soon learned, it can also be stifling.

It wasn't all discipline and drudgery, though. I was assigned to the RAF band, where I played the euphonium. Playing with that band was the high point of my time in the Air Force. I do believe that the basic training I received was the one thing that I benefited from the most during my time in the RAF, even though, on the surface, it had nothing to do with music. That training is responsible, in large part, for shaping me into the disciplined and hardworking person that I eventually became. It's something that I wish every young man and woman had the opportunity to experience today. I truly believe that it would change our world for the better.

I spent six months in the RAF before accepting that it simply wasn't for me. The bandleader ordered me to stop playing the piano and concentrate on the Euphonium. That didn't sit right with me. Piano was my first love, musically speaking. I decided to leave and pursue my passion. At the time, the structured military lifestyle and an unpredictable future as a musician seemed diametrically opposed to one another. And in many ways, of course, they were. An aspiring musician's life can be chaotic. That's part of the bohemian allure of the lifestyle, but it's also terribly daunting. Once you get established and make a name for yourself, things start to settle down and become more orderly, but that outcome is by no means a sure thing. A lot of musicians flame out or never find their footing. That this fate did not befall me is creditable, at least partly, to the basic training I had put myself through. In that sense, the world of the RAF recruit and the world of the starving musician are not so incompatible after all. Talent and passion can only get you part of the way. Grit, determination, and discipline will keep you pushing yourself long after you feel you've hit your limit.

Right out of the RAF, I started working as a salesperson at Forsyth's Music Shop on Deansgate in Manchester. It was an entry-level job, and it was only remotely related to what I wanted to be doing, but I knew that I was putting myself in a position where I would be able to make connections and keep my finger on the pulse of the local music scene. Any work that got me more entrenched in that culture, I figured, had to be a step in the right direction. And sure enough, it opened up a whole new world of music for me. We supplied strings, reeds, and other accessories to the Halle Orchestra, and I was able to learn a great deal about the classical music industry and how other areas of the music industry functioned.

Forsyth's was merely my day job, however. I also worked at the Lake Hotel near Belle Vue at night. I was the organist, and I formed one half of a duo with a drummer called Steve Martin. Wow, did we have fun! In a time and place where many club organ and drum duos were playing "Roll Out the Barrel" and "White Cliffs of Dover," Steve and I were killing it with a *loud* medley from *Jesus Christ Superstar*. It was an amazing place to hone my craft, and I had an absolute blast! You could tell from studying the crowd's reaction, night after night, that what we were doing was a breath of fresh air. Knowing what people want, and how to give it to them, was a skill I picked up early on, and it's a skill that's every bit as important as actual musical proficiency if you want to get ahead. Truth be told, though, there were times when the audience was the last thing on my mind. There were nights when I got so lost in the songs that Steve and I were playing that our listeners entirely dropped away. It's an incredible feeling--one that every musician can relate to, I'm sure.

The Lake Hotel was a popular venue for live music, and I had the opportunity to play with some fantastic entertainers. These experiences were invaluable in helping me develop my skills and make inroads within the music industry. So many spectacular people came and went through the Lake Hotel's doors. People brimming with talent, humor, and intelligence. Some were there to perform; some were just there to enjoy the show. I am once again faced with the impossible task of trying to recount them all. It simply can't be done. There isn't enough space, and some of their names and faces have sadly been lost to time. One young comedian I befriended was Georgie Peorgie, who later changed his stage name to George King.

We are still in touch today and often reminisce about those beginning days of our careers. I often think just how cool it would be if we had something like Facebook back in those days. Some impossibly huge scrapbook that would trigger those long-lost memories. Just writing this book makes me realize that there are so many people and so many things that I have forgotten. Ah…the ravages of time!

I mention this wish of mine to have all those missing memories restored in order to make a point. There are a handful of people I met at the Lake Hotel who touched me so deeply, and whose lives became so intertwined with my own, that I could never forget them if I lived for a thousand years. The Lake Hotel, you see, was where I met Strawberry Pye, a brother and sister act consisting of Ann and

Phil Stevenson on bass and guitar, respectively, in addition to Dave Merriman on drums. I had been working at the Lake Hotel for a while and had already played with a number of stellar musicians before Strawberry Pye came along, but they stood out to me immediately. They were a very seventies group, and I thought they were absolutely brilliant! I was particularly taken with Ann, who struck me as incredibly sexy and pretty. But there was also a certain docility and timidness to her that I didn't understand, given how vivacious I found her, especially when she was performing. It was a quality that she shared with her brother Phil--and it wouldn't be long before I learned just where it came from.

I couldn't have known it at the time, but Strawberry Pye would swiftly become a pivotal part of my life, one that would shape my personality for years to come. I had come of age with a whole slew of memorable school chums and wonderful musicians, but Ann, Phil, and Dave would prove to be the people who walked with me across the threshold between adolescence and adulthood. They were the ones with whom I first forged my musical identity and achieved real independence. But this was by no means an easy feat, for reasons I could never have anticipated.

CHAPTER 5:
WALKABOUT

Young love is blind to the perils and pitfalls that await it
—unknown

* * *

I quickly formed a friendship with the members of Strawberry Pye, and I was both thrilled and more than a little flattered when they asked me to join them on keyboards. It was an exciting opportunity, and I was eager to see where it would take me. Immediately my imagination began running wild, not only with all the things that the band might do for me, but also all the things that I could do for the band. I had a clear enough head, even back in those heady days, to be able to tell that Strawberry Pye, while a very promising act, had yet to achieve its full potential. Perhaps, I thought, my contributions could propel it a little further along, and together the four of us could really start to make something of ourselves.

It was all incredibly exhilarating. Joining Strawberry Pye was like receiving a sudden infusion of love into my life that was enough to very nearly overload my system. Love for the music we were playing, as well as love for Ann, the hip, pretty bassist, with whom I instantly became besotted. What I can see clearly now, and what I think I must have suspected at the time, is that those two loves were so tangled up together that there was really no telling where one ended and the other began. I fell in love with the band and with Ann, at more or less the same instant. And I fell hard for them both. I think the romantic connections that form between impassioned young artists have to be among the most intense in the world--particularly if they happen to be collaborating on the same project. I'd imagine that actors conducting an affair backstage in the days leading up to opening night, must feel something akin to the same rush that I felt. You go out there in front of the audience, alongside the love of your life, and you put on the best show that you can, and the adrenaline kick lingers long after the curtain has fallen and the sound of the applause has faded. It carries you through the quieter, more private hours after everyone's gone home, making those intimate experiences feel just as momentous and as grandiose as the time you spent standing side by side in the spotlight.

Ann was great looking, and young, and I was very taken with the way she sang. She was perhaps not a first-rate instrumentalist, unlike her brother Phil, but she was a good singer, and she looked terrific, and the energy that she brought to the band was a significant asset. The appeal of a pop band is seldom solely reducible to its members' musical prowess. If there's chemistry between the performers, that can make a huge difference--and chemistry was one thing that Ann and I most definitely had in spades, though we did what we could to conceal it from her brother. Our physical relationship began very shortly after I joined the band, but it took a long time for us to let that cat out of the bag. We didn't want our romance to get in the way of the music--or, if worst came to worst, to precipitate the band's breakup. But Ann and I were infatuated with one another, and our poker faces couldn't have been all that refined at that point in our lives. Maybe it was more of an open secret--or maybe it's the case that Phil didn't see it because he didn't wish to see it. Regardless, we went about things clandestinely for several months. Far from impeding our mutual infatuation, the secrecy might have done something to invigorate it. If there's anything more passionate than an affair between two young people with a shared creative dream, it's a forbidden affair between those two people under those same circumstances.

We were both seventeen. In that regard, the emotional highs that we were hitting were fairly typical, though they felt anything but ordinary to us at the time. I think that we both thought that we were deeply in love with one another. But we were kids, needless to say. Everything was brand new to us. And there's no question that some of our exaggerated emotions came from the environment that we were living in. Young lovers can't help but get in over their heads, at the best of times. Add to that timeless truth the fact that we happened to be in a band operating in the UK music scene of the 1970s, and you can toss any hint of regret or reticence out the window. It felt as though our every action was steeped in enthusiasm, sincerity, and a sense of our own potential. I wanted us to go about everything--even our secret relationship--unashamed. The only way forward, it seemed to me, was to throw ourselves, body and soul, into whatever we did, with nothing held back.

There was another factor, a far less glamorous one, that also contributed to the outsize feelings that Ann and I were experiencing, while simultaneously posing a threat to our momentum as a band and the freedom I desired for myself. As I became more involved with Strawberry Pye, I began to see that there were deeper, darker issues at play in Ann and Phil's family life. Their parents were controlling and overbearing to a degree that made me uncomfortable from the word go--and my discomfort would only ratchet up as time wore on. Their mother, in particular, was something of a puppet master where her children were concerned. When I first started to get a feel for her pathology, I was a bit confused and taken aback. I had begun to brace myself for one problem, only to find myself faced with a different and more insidious one. What I expected was a straight-laced, traditional control freak who would try to quash Ann and Phil's musical ambitions and force them onto a more orthodox career path. Instead, what I was up against, I soon realized, was a woman who did, in fact, want her children to keep playing music--but only on her terms and strictly for her benefit.

Ann and Phil's parents ran both the band and their lives, sponging off their children to an extent that I found truly distasteful. Their father did all the driving, ferrying them to and from gigs, but beyond that, they were content to sit back and reap the benefits of their children's labors. As a relative outsider, I was able to see the situation with unclouded eyes. It was an oppressive and unhealthy environment, and I knew at once that it wasn't tenable in the long term. But Ann and Phil had grown accustomed to their parents' parasitism over the years, and their complacency, combined with my devotion to Ann, was enough to get me to ignore the warning signs. Given the choice between my head and my heart, I went with the latter. What can I say? That's what it is to be young and smitten.

It was both financially and psychologically draining. We were working every night, doing different gigs (every last one of which Ann and Phil's mother had to approve of in advance) and forking over our earnings. All we had to show for ourselves was the satisfaction of a job well done--which is not worthless when you're just starting out. But it's not something that you can subsist on. We were never able to strike out on our own--which, of course, is just the way Ann and Phil's parents wanted it. Because my two bandmates had been laboring under this toxic status quo for some time before I came along, it was difficult to make them appreciate just how iniquitous it was. And because I was carrying on a romantic relationship with Ann in the midst of all this, I had a strong incentive to not rock the boat too much. I didn't want to lose her, and I wasn't confident that, if push came to shove, she would choose the band––and, by extension, me––over her parents.

In spite of all these challenges, we were able to eke out a string of small successes, night after night, culminating in the release of a double-A side record. Seeing a record emblazoned with the name "Strawberry Pye," and being able to hold my own music in my hands, felt like a major milestone to me as a teenager. Phil wrote a song called "It's Too Late," and I wrote a song called "Walkabout." As I write this, I find myself wishing, not for the first time, that I still had a copy of that track.

CHAPTER 6:
WHAT UNCLE HARRY TAUGHT ME

An uncle is someone you can look up to, no matter how tall you grow
—Unknown

* * *

My attitude toward Ann and Phil's family, and the unease with which I regarded its abusive power imbalances, was undoubtedly informed by a drama within my own family that unfolded around this same period. A drama that I have yet to touch on.

When I was serving in the RAF, I received word, quite out of the blue, that my parents were separating. Their divorce created shock waves within our extended family more so than for me personally. I was out of the house and endeavoring to be my own man by that point, and I had largely shed the desire to be parented. For that reason, I didn't need my Mum and Dad to keep functioning the same way they had when I was a boy. I appreciated them for staying together for my sake, and my siblings' sake, for as long as they did, in spite of whatever interpersonal problems they'd had. Nevertheless, the split did manage to leave some scars on my psyche, in addition to underscoring a longstanding grudge. My father, unsurprisingly, didn't fight it. From what I understand, my mother asked him for a divorce, and that was that. His chronic fear of confrontation had once again gotten the better of him, at one of the most pivotal junctures in his life. That did bother me.

I couldn't entirely blame him for being cowed by the situation, however. There were extenuating circumstances that would have defeated many men in his position––circumstances which I'm going to try to discuss with as much delicacy as I can.

My mother had fallen for, and eventually wound up marrying, one of my cousins on my father's side of the family. His name was Eric. You can imagine the difficulties and familial fissures that this created for us all across multiple generations. I managed to stay out of it, for the most part, even after exiting the Air Force. But no one in my family, on either side, was able to escape the fallout entirely unscathed.

It was complicated as hell. I could see thorny emotions taking root in many of my relatives, some of whom were, on the face of it, even further removed from the situation than I was.

Because all of this transpired when I was a young adult, and because I made a choice early on to try and be as charitable and nonjudgmental as possible to all the parties involved, I'd say that I emerged from the whole scandal relatively well-adjusted. I can't credit that solely to my own good sense, however. I had a role model in my life who showed me how to weather the storm––one whose absence from these pages, up until now, must be corrected immediately. His influence on me in my early years cannot possibly be overstated.

As fate would have it, the current date, as I sit here, typing away and sipping my coffee, is February 14th, 2024. This is the day my uncle Harry would have turned 86. Why does that date strike me as significant? He was only an uncle, after all. Yes and no. To me, he was always a great deal more than that. Something much closer to a second father or a beloved friend. I could apply any number of honorary labels to him, but the point is simply this: he was one of the most important figures in my life, and he remains so, even after his passing. I could not have loved him any more than I did.

When I was a youngster, I always eagerly looked forward to visits from Uncle Harry and Auntie Barbara. Harry was my father's brother, and he and Barbara had two kids together, my cousins Stephen and Karen. Each time the four of them would swing by, we would always have a wonderful time. There were occasions when we dropped in on them at their place when I was growing up, but it's the times we spent under my parents' roof that I remember most vividly. I have innumerable memories of Harry walking through the door, beckoning me over, and asking me to show him what progress I had made on the piano. "Alright," he would say to me. "Sit down, and show me what you can do." He had a genuine interest in me and my piano studies, and it showed. You could tell that his belief in me, as well as his desire to make me feel good, both came from a sincere place. The man really gave a damn. That's why those memories remain so vivid for me, even now.

As I started to get older and continued to refine my skills, he got into the habit of telling me that the only way he would be able to gauge my progress, the only yardstick he would ever understand, was how well I could play "MacArthur Park," which was his favorite tune. It became a running joke between the two of us, one that we laughed about for years.

Harry was a long-distance lorry driver all through my childhood. Much of his time was spent on the road. I got to see him, at most, once a month. He delivered petrol for Esso, which was one of the largest oil and gas companies in the UK at that time, with a fleet of drivers responsible for transporting fuel across the country. Esso drivers were known for their distinctive uniforms and trucks, often emblazoned with the company's iconic tiger logo. The job of an Esso driver was physically and mentally grueling, requiring long, sleepless hours behind the wheel, and the ability to navigate narrow, winding streets and country roads. Despite the challenges, many drivers took pride in their work and in the role they played in keeping the country's economy moving––none more so than my uncle. In the early 1970s, in a nationwide competition, he was voted Driver of the Year. That impressed me when I was young, and it still impresses me to this day!

As I mentioned, when my mother remarried, it was to one of my father's nephews. One of Harry's nephews, in other words. But in spite of his proximity to it, Harry appeared to take the scandal in stride. Certainly, it never came between him and me, even as it was creating a storm of recriminations and shifting allegiances across both sides of the family. He didn't allow it to fluster him or interfere with the familial bonds that he held dear. All the ill will that was swirling around us didn't seem to touch him, and so I decided that I wouldn't let it touch me either. Were it not for the example that he set, I would not have been capable of handling my parents' separation in such a clear-eyed and compassionate way––and, further down the road, I would not have been able to see Ann and Phil's family for what it was. As contentious and awkward as my parents' divorce was, it was still a vastly preferable state of affairs to the world of constant scrutiny and exploitation that Ann and Phil had grown up in. Seeing how their parents comported themselves made me view my own mom and Dad in a more favorable light. But then, I was already primed to see them that way––because Uncle Harry showed me how.

I've lost many loved ones over the years. It's an inevitable part of the aging process, though acknowledging that doesn't do all that much to ease the pain. Harry is at the forefront of my mind, I suppose, because he's only just passed recently at the time of this writing. He died in December of last year, just a couple of months shy of his 86th birthday. Despite the infrequency with which I saw him in my youth, he made a deep and lasting impression on me and did so much to sculpt my worldview. He and I remained close when it seemed like our entire family was breaking up and crashing down around our ears. I'll have more to say about him and how our relationship evolved as this book goes on. I mention him now because he was integral to my experience of my parents' divorce, and my perception of my parents' divorce played a key role in what comes next. I had internalized a lesson that many children of divorce take to heart: sometimes, separation is for the best.

That was the thought that was on my mind the night that I decided I could not allow Ann and Phil's parents to keep bleeding us dry. A breakup doesn't necessarily have to break *you*. That's what I've found. The right breakup at the right time, can leave you stronger than you ever were before.

CHAPTER 7:
THE EMANCIPATION OF
STRAWBERRY PYE

Don't take any shit from anybody
—Billy Joel

* * *

Rarely in my life have I felt more keenly aware of a cloud of toxicity hanging over my head than I was during the early days of Strawberry Pye. It was more than I could take--and I wasn't the only one. Dave left the band after a while, and I have to assume that his departure was at least partly motivated by the constraints imposed upon us by Ann and Phil's parents. We hired a new drummer, Ernie Barrow, and didn't let the disruption trip us up too much.

Still, losing Dave was something of a wake-up call, at least for me. How much longer was I going to stick around? How many drummers would I watch come and go, while I gritted my teeth and silently endured the sponging and micromanaging? I felt a loyalty to Ann and I couldn't see myself simply walking out on the band. But I also knew that I wouldn't be able to grin and bear it forever—hell, I had only managed to bite my tongue around Jim Fontaine for about a gig and a half. It was only a matter of time before my anger and my pride bubbled to the surface. Conflict was inevitable. Eventually, I would have to prove to myself, once again, that I was not a pushover.

The band was doing great, but our private lives were worsening by the day. It felt like we were living in a prison. I resented this intensely and resented myself for putting up with it, even in the short term, even for the sake of my friend and my girlfriend. We were supposed to be bandmates, not cellmates. It seemed to me that I had traded the suffocating stringency of military life for a different and less dignified form of servitude. Not all authority figures are deserving of respect and deference by default. Ann and Phil's mother didn't think twice or lose a wink of sleep over her treatment of us. Every cent that we earned was hers. This, of course, is not a relationship that you would ever tolerate from any manager, unless blood ties and inborn love were messing with your judgment. In effect, she was picking my pocket and taking food out of the mouths of her children—and, worse still, she was utterly unbothered by this arrangement. It made perfect sense to her. There was no shame, no self-awareness. Left to her own devices, she would have gone on like this, leaning on us and filching from us indefinitely. The change had to come from below if it was going to happen at all. It had to come from me.

As was the case with the fateful Jim Fontaine blowup, I have not held onto the details of the straw that broke the camel's back. If it hadn't been one thing, it would have been another. I wonder if Ann and Phil's parents were aware, at the time, of the kind of powder keg that they were sitting on. They were, ostensibly, the adults in the room. It stands to reason that they should have been able to see the writing on the wall if I could. Maybe their children's exodus came as a surprise to them, and maybe it didn't. Nothing in the world could have been less surprising to me.

We managed to secure a summer season in The Isle Of Man, near Summerland, which meant that we were going to have at least a number of weeks, if not months, away from the parents. When it was over, Phil decided to stay in the Isle Of Man. He was done with the Drama…and he followed in Dave's footsteps…the band was no more. I gave Ann an ultimatum, of sorts. We were at a crossroads, and I laid out for her what our options were, as I saw it. Either we left ourselves at the mercy of their parents, at the cost of our music and our mental health, or we severed ties with them. I don't remember precisely how I put it – or if it was a joint decision - I like to think that I was gentle as I felt I could be, under the circumstances, given my mounting outrage at the injustice of it all. We had been playing when they told us, and traveling where they told us, for far too long. Ann knew, deep down, that it was overly restrictive and unfair, but she was tolerant of it, and I wasn't. We were making good money and seeing next to none of it. It was high time that somebody spoke up.

That's how I led Ann to leave her home. For me, it was simply the latest in a long line of sudden upsets and decisive choices. You could draw a straight line from me standing up to Jim Fontaine, to me leaving the RAF, to me freeing Strawberry Pye––or what was left of it–– from its shackles. For Ann and Phil, fleeing the proverbial nest was necessarily more complex, and harder to come to terms with. But there's no doubt in my mind that it was the right decision for everyone––including Ann and Phil's parents, who never would have stopped scrounging off their children if someone hadn't come along and slapped their hands away. It was no way for us to live, and it was no way for them to live, either.

Bear in mind that I was still dating Ann in secret. I can't know how her feelings for me entered into her thinking when she chose to prioritize the band's future over her relationship with her family. We loved one another (or thought we did), and we loved performing. And I, for one, loved freedom––and I was confident that I could teach her to love it as well. So it was love, ultimately, that led us out of the purgatory of Ann's parents' house and into the real world. A confusing, multifaceted mass of love, with many moving parts. It was like stepping out of the darkness and into the light. Ann and I stopped keeping our relationship under wraps, for one thing. I've frequently joked over the years that Strawberry Pye, under her parents' management, reminded me of nothing so much as the book *Flowers in the Attic*. The fear and trepidation, the noxious creepiness of their whole family dynamic, the sense of everything being shrouded in secrecy––the way that you had to resort to keeping secrets, whether you liked it or not, just to be able to set foot in their house––that was the dark atmosphere that Ann's parents created. Their mother was the main culprit, but she couldn't have pushed it as far as she did without their father's complicity. I was happy to be rid of them both––and so were Ann and Phil, though I'm sure that their happiness could not have been as simple and as unfettered as mine.

Once I dragged them away from all that, and we started living our own lives, we had no choice but to start running our own affairs. Ann and I ended up getting a flat together in a place called Hattersley, near Glossop. Ours was a very bare existence, for a good long while. There never was much cash to go around. We were living on beans on toast (which is a very British way of saying that we were living on the bread line). We'd have a loaf of bread and a few cans of beans, and we'd portion them out, one slice and spoonful at a time, taking care to make them last as long as humanly possible. But we were finally independent, and that was priceless. Seeing Ann come out of her shell, not just onstage, but in her personal life, confirmed for me that we had made the right call. After a very short time, we reconnected with Phil and it didn't take long before we all knew that it was time for Strawberry Pye to reform. It wasn't a long break, but it sure felt good to be back together. Phil lived somewhere else at the time and was dating a girl from Fallowfield called Karen. It was an incredibly positive period for the three of us and even though we were just barely getting by, at times, the good that came from our emancipation from their parents was amazing. We were able to travel further and take more risks. The money we made was often meager, and it quickly got swallowed up by bills and expenses. But it was entirely ours.

I have to confess, I don't have as much insight as I'd like into how Ann and Phil felt during all of this. I just know that we were all happy--never more so than when we were performing. Playing music together always made the bad times more bearable, both in the beginning, when we were dealing with Ann and Phil's parents, and later on when we were coping with the stressors that come with independence.

Even in this celebratory state of mind, however, I was conscious of the fact that this was not the end of my story. There was still a spirit of restlessness in me, a yearning to do and see more. The disintegration of my parents' marriage, followed by the breakaway from Ann and Phil's parents, had left me with a sense of loss and liberation, of family structures crumbling away, of being cut loose and left to forge my own path in a world in which anything was possible. It was as though I was standing amid a pile of rubble after a great collapse--but I had been granted a beautiful, unobstructed view of the open sky.

CHAPTER 8:
A THREE-PIECE BAND

The music business is a cruel and shallow money trench, a long plastic
hallway where thieves and pimps run free, and good men die like dogs.
There's also a negative side — **Hunter S. Thompson**

* * *

Strawberry Pye truly hit its stride in the years following our split from Ann and Phil's
parents. We were more adventurous, more carefree, and more successful than ever.
Getting Ann and Phil's parents out of the picture wasn't just good for our mental
well-being (though that would have been reason enough by itself). I'm convinced that
our music also improved. We never would have been able to find our voice with the
two of them standing on our throats. I got to know Phil better once we were all living
on our own, and I gradually came to realize that he was not only a great bandmate,
but also a true entertainer. He had an incredible ability to connect with an audience
and engage them in a way that few performers can. I'm able to appreciate now, in a
way that I don't think I was able to in my early twenties, how much I learned from
him during the time we spent sharing the stage. I had always been closer with Ann
than her brother, for obvious reasons, but the passage of time, and the act of putting on shows together, deepened my friendship with Phil to a degree I hadn't seen
coming. It got to a point where I had no doubt that he and I would remain friends,
even if the band were to break up. This confidence, unfortunately, did not extend to
my relationship with Ann.

I can't say precisely how it happened. Maybe Ann missed her parents more
than I realized--while that's hard for me to imagine. A mutual disenchantment
seemed to set in, so slowly as to sneak up on me. I had created a scenario for the two
of us, free of her parents and their parasitic ways, in which limitless happiness seemed
close at hand. And we were happy together. As time went on, however, our happiness
began to feel more muted and constrained. It wasn't the bills, or the gigs, or any other
material problem I could point to. We were handling all of that. The thrill just went

out of our relationship. That kind of dispassion is difficult for a musician to face up to, I've found. It's the furthest thing from the kind of energy you're trying to foster when you're jamming onstage. And even in your private life, it feels wrong and out of place. Almost as though you've flubbed the song you're playing somewhere. You don't know quite what went wrong--all you know is that you've lost the audience. That's how I would describe the way things ended with Ann. You might say that we were hitting the right notes, but we weren't making music.

We sort of just fell apart. There never came a night when one of us turned to the other and said, "I've had it, it's over." It wasn't a clean break--and I'm now realizing that, in that regard, it was without major precedent in my life. Nothing could have felt more final, more definitive, than how I walked out on The Fontaines, or the RAF, or Ann and Phil's parents. Parting ways with Ann, on the other hand, was sort of fuzzy around the edges, and frustratingly indefinite. The long and the short of it is that Ann left the band, and I left Ann. It sounds simple enough when I put it that way. But it played out with terrible slowness, and so many things were left unsaid. A failing relationship is the sort of thing that tends to bring out the worst in everyone. I can at least say that there weren't any painful arguments, as things drew to a close. We managed to avoid all that unpleasantness, and so my memories of Ann are almost entirely positive.

Ann's departure from Strawberry Pye did not break up the rest of us, though we did cease to exist as a four-piece. Ernie, Phil, and I were all committed to the craft in a way that she had never been, so we sensed that we still had a future as a band, even if it wasn't the future we had originally envisioned. Decisions had to be made as to what we wanted to sound like, and what sort of group we wanted to be. There was no shortage of opportunities to ply our trade and hash out our style. New gigs were seldom hard to come by. Our greatest opportunity to date soon arrived in the form of Butlin's, a chain of holiday camps that operated in, among other places, Filey, England and Ayr, Scotland (both of which various permutations of the band would eventually go on to play). Our first Butlin's engagement was to be the biggest stage we had ever played on, and we all knew going in that it would either prove to be our loftiest triumph or our most crushing failure.

Butlin's was, to put it simply, life-changing. We played there for four summer seasons in the seventies. One in Filey and 3 in Ayr.

We had our own show at the Beachcomber Bar five or six nights a week, and also accompanied late-night cabaret on Wednesdays. That was such an important time for me. A breakthrough moment in more ways than one. It took Strawberry Pye to a different level, and it took me to a different level, too. I got to work, for the first time in my life, with a lot of famous TV stars, accompanying them during their acts.

The fact that I was able to sight-read music very well led to an influx of job opportunities that was enough to make my head spin. One of the men that I was lucky enough to network with was Pat O'Hare, who did more to alter the trajectory of my life than just about anyone else I could name.

For Strawberry Pye, as well as for me, there was before Butlin's, and there was after Butlin's. The excitement of those days, the unflagging energy and enthusiasm that we brought to our songs, was a rare and precious thing. It was during this time that I co-wrote a song with Roger Edwards and what would become a signature tune for Gerry the Tramp--a nonsensical ditty called "My Dad's a Fridge." The melody was rather simple, and the lyrics were outlandish, but I suppose they must have been catchy and memorable enough, because the song became a hit at Butlin's, and people left the resort singing it for weeks after its debut. One thing's for sure, an artist can't control what strikes a chord with people and what doesn't. If you'd told me, when I was scribbling those crazy words down, that they were going to form a key part of my musical legacy, I would have said you were mental. But life, as they say, is full of surprises.

Our time at Butlin's was about much more than just performing as a means of making ends meet. We dimly understood that truth at the time, the three of us--and I, for one, can see it with perfect clarity now. Butlin's was about connecting with people, having fun, and enjoying the experience of making music together. In the end, that's what it's all about--sharing your passion and connecting with others through the power of music. I still talk with Phil every now and again. We can't help but reminisce about the good old days, even when we try to confine ourselves to the present. We'll start talking about what is happening in our lives these days, and before you know it, we're back at Butlin's. Why fight it? If you'd been there, you'd understand. There was nothing quite like performing in the UK club scene in the 1970s.

CHAPTER 9:
FRONTMEN AND SIDEMEN

The best teacher is experience and not through someone's distorted point of view —**Jack Kerouac**

* * *

I encourage you to hop on Google when you get the chance if you're curious to see what Butlin's was like back in the seventies and eighties. After a minute or two of scrolling, you'll have a pretty good idea of the kind of place it was. The old photos will paint a fuller picture for you than I can. Thousands of people came and went during its peak seasons, staying in small chalets, dining, dancing, and taking part in all sorts of activities. Calling it a vacation destination doesn't do it justice. Every night at the Beachcomber we played for about four or five hours to a crowd of roughly two thousand people. I don't know how long it would have taken for the novelty of all that to wear off, and for a sense of drudgery to start to set in. More than four summer seasons, I know that much, because that's how long we spent working there. Butlin's was a lot of things, but it was never, ever "been there, done that." Even when you were playing the same old set in the same old bar, listening to the drunken holidaymakers singing the chorus of "My Dad's a Fridge" at you for the fiftieth time, there was a freshness and newness to all of it. Mind you, I couldn't have been a day over 21. That helped.

I want to give you a little taste of the size of the place, how packed it was, and how young and overwhelmed I was, so that you can appreciate what it would take for someone to stand out from the crowd. Strawberry Pye, at this point, was three guys. All good friends, and all single. We were always seeing unfamiliar faces in the audience. Every day there was a steady stream of vacationers coming in, and a steady stream of vacationers going out. Phil, Ernie, and I wanted nothing more than to dazzle them all--and to put the moves on about half of them, give or take, if they would have us. The two questions on my mind, at all times, were simply this: *Who's leaving today? Who's arriving today?* We kept so busy, and the guests came and went so quickly, that tantalizing opportunities for acquaintanceship were constantly slipping through our fingers. Nevertheless, we did get to meet a lot of incredible people. I dated a dancer called Susan Colquhoun. She had recently ended a relationship with a Scottish entertainer named Jimmy Nairn—a very talented musician and uproarious comedian in the 1970s. Fast forward 20 years, and Jimmy and I grew closer, working on shows together in the 1990's, and remain close friends to this day!

Another person I met—the one who touched me the most deeply—was a musician named Eileen. Strawberry Pye was always in high demand at Butlin's. And that stands to reason. We put on a good show, played a lot of upbeat dance stuff, and knew how to work the crowd. But to be frank, there were a lot of acts at Butlin's in those days who could make a similar claim, and they weren't all as popular as we were. Our somewhat unique selling point was that all three of us could read music. This meant that we could always be relied upon to accompany the guest artists. Management could shove us onstage in a pinch, if they had to, no matter who was playing, secure in the knowledge that we wouldn't make fools of ourselves. We played with some big stars, and also a lot of local acts. One of these local acts was a duo from Glasgow called Us Two, comprised of a pair of sisters. I would wager that the younger of the two girls was about 25 or so, while Eileen—the older sister—was closer to 34. She and I kicked off an affair not long after the first night that we accompanied Us Two, which was brief, intense, and unforgettable. It was a perfect fit, in other words, for the backdrop of Butlin's.

Romantic affairs at Butlin's could often be quick and haphazard, and they frequently went nowhere. The first thing you had to do was determine whether the person you had your eye on was single. Eileen was. The rest took care of itself, in this case. It felt effortless. So much so that it was tempting to believe that what we had together was true love. Whatever it was, it brought a swift end to my Butlin's bachelorhood. No more eyeing the attractive new arrivals with Phil and Ernie. But that was fine by me. I was enraptured by Eileen. My romance with Ann had been essentially adolescent. Ours had been a secret relationship for long stretches, specifically because we didn't want her parents to get wind of it, as we knew they wouldn't approve. Needless to say, Eileen had aged out of having to sneak around, and she no longer felt much need to solicit her mom and Dad's approval. It had been one thing to win the heart of a musician my own age, a woman with whom I shared innumerable youthful foibles. But when Eileen fell for me, I suddenly felt as though I was not just a promising upstart, but rather a full-fledged adult, with something real to offer. I could picture myself in ten years, still coming back to Butlin's, still knocking them dead, just like she was doing. I wasn't sure if Phil and Ernie were going to have that same longevity, or where they would fit in going forward. I just knew that I, at least, wasn't going to be some flash in the pan.

What began as an impulsive Butlin's fling rapidly progressed to something a lot more substantial. When Strawberry Pye left Butlin's at the end of that first season, Eileen and I vowed to make things work between us, even though she was headed back to Glasgow. My life became a whirlwind of concerts and travel, an unending succession of venues that all bled together, and roads that I got to know like the back of my hand. I used to drive up to Glasgow from Manchester on Sunday, steal a couple of days with Eileen, then hit the road again, arriving back in Manchester just in time for this or that gig. It would have been maddening, were it not for the fact that I was madly in love.

The following season, Eileen and I both found ourselves back at Butlin's. A year had passed, and our relationship seemed to be going stronger than ever. So we took what seemed to us to be the logical next step: we got engaged. In hindsight, this was a terrible decision, but at the time it felt natural enough. It wouldn't have been customary, back in those days, for the woman to propose to the man, but my memory of it is that Eileen was pushing for the engagement more so than I was, even if I was the one who formally popped the question. I don't know why I did it, to be entirely honest. I was wild about Eileen––but not wild enough, it would seem, to completely cure myself of my cold feet. Even though we'd been together for a year, it all struck me as a bit too soon, too sudden. But my words and my nerve failed me, just as they had with Ann.

It was during this period, playing music in Manchester nonstop, taking whatever work came along, that I first started to get a taste for the life of a professional sideman. I wasn't dragging Phil and Ernie along to all of my gigs––and they certainly weren't tagging along on my treks up to Glasgow. We started to do our own things and see less and less of each other, even though the band hadn't officially been dissolved. The notion of Strawberry Pye having a future was beginning to feel increasingly unimportant to me. It had already changed so much from when I had first come aboard as a teenage keyboardist. There are musicians out there whose egos mandate that they have a singular act with which they're associated--ideally, one in which they're always front and center. Jim Fontaine had been like that. But my brain wasn't wired that way. I didn't care if I never became a frontman, so long as I was able to foster some kind of future for myself as a musician. I could even live with the death of Strawberry Pye, if it came to that, provided there was no bad blood between Phil, Ernie, and myself. And I'm happy to say there never was.

Bit by bit, preserving Strawberry Pye became less of a priority for us. It's not that we lost our enthusiasm--rather, our enthusiasm continued to ramp up, to the point where it could no longer be contained within a single act with a defined style and sound. The real glory of music hasn't to do with having a band that you can call your own and slap your name on. Playing music whenever and wherever you can--that's glorious. It was a glory that I was about to hurl myself headlong into.

CHAPTER 10:
THE STRANGE PULL

Let yourself be silently drawn by the strange pull of what you really love.
It will not lead you astray — **Rumi**

* * *

As a sideman, I had the opportunity to play with a wide range of musicians, each with their own unique style and sound. I shared the stage with so many amazing entertainers, from the raucous comedy of Cannon & Ball, to the crazed antics of Tommy Cooper, to the soulful harmonies of The Stylistics. I was perpetually being challenged to adapt my playing to fit the needs of each artist, and it was a challenge that I relished. The pinnacle for me, without a doubt, was playing with Gladys Knight. I can only describe that show as a dream come true. I was so starstruck that my number one priority was staying out of her way. What a force of nature that woman was. She was one of the most talented and dedicated performers I have ever met, and it was an honor to share the stage with her. I didn't know then if Eileen and I would ever have kids together but I found myself thinking, as I walked offstage after the Gladys Knight show, that if children were in the cards for us, then at least now I had a story I could impress them with.

Eileen and I were still engaged when I got a call from Pat O'Hare that completely blew the future that she and I were imagining out of the water. He asked me, point blank, if I had any interest in going to Spain. And not just for a show, or a season or two, but for steady, long-term work. There was an opening for a musical entertainer at a beachside vacation resort. He needed my answer as soon as I could muster one up. I thought I must have misheard him. It was a ludicrous idea, but one that I could not get out of my head. I was twenty-two years old, and I was on my feet, holding down a job that every musician in Manchester wanted, with impending nuptials on the horizon. Only a fool would toss all of that aside after receiving a random phone call, no matter how seductive Pat's job offer was.

And yet, that's precisely what I did. I threw it all away.

It couldn't have possibly been an easy decision. But it felt easier to me, at that age, than it had any right to feel. Deep down, I sensed that it was the right thing to do. I broke off my engagement, quit my job, and moved to Spain. Something was drawing me across the water. As satisfying as it was to be making a comfortable living and climbing the ladder in the Manchester music scene, I saw a ceiling for myself there that I did not see when I thought about the wider world beyond. Maybe I was worried, rightly or wrongly, that I'd never be able to top playing a show with Gladys Knight--certainly, I was worried that Pat O'Hare would have second thoughts, and offer the hotel job to someone else, someone older and more worldly than myself, if I dallied too long. I didn't much feel like hemming and hawing, anyway. Ever since my first introduction to the green fields of Glossop when I was a boy, I had understood the allure of faraway places and foreign cultures. Pat's offer, random as it was, was simply too good to pass up.

It pains me to admit this, but it was harder for me to leave my career in Manchester than it was to leave my fiance. I don't know if I had fallen out of love with Eileen, or if the affection I felt for her had always been less profound than what she felt for me. I still cared for her deeply, but somewhere along the line I had stopped cherishing her the way that a man is supposed to cherish his wife. I told her--quite bluntly, I'm afraid--that something had come up, and that I was bound for Spain, and that it was over. Ending things with her so unceremoniously was cruel of me, and I have nothing to say in my defense--other than that marrying her, with the reservations I was feeling, would have been crueler still. Nonetheless, I don't feel good about the way I handled things. It was much too reminiscent of the weaselly way in which I had broken things off with Ann. Sometimes, in life, you have to learn the same lesson twice before it sticks. My sense of shame was mounting, after these two clumsy breakups--I knew that there would never be a third like that. This personal vow of mine didn't do Eileen any good, but I did manage to keep it. I've not seen or spoken to her since. It was a significant, bittersweet part of my life, and it's over. It ended just as suddenly as it began.

I'm not sorry that my sense of adventure won out over my common sense. I had a hunch then, one that has been vindicated by time, that I had no choice but to take the opportunity Pat had presented to me, if I wanted to keep growing as a musician. Still, on paper, it didn't make a whole lot of sense. The money wasn't great, and I didn't know a soul in Spain. But something was telling me to go. And god, am I glad I listened.

The last thing I did, before making up my mind for good, was to go to my father and ask him for his two cents. I wasn't expecting that conversation to do much to tip the scales one way or the other, to be honest. My old man had never been one to take any big risks or stray outside his comfort zone--much to my disappointment, at various points in my upbringing. I half-expected him to admonish me for even entertaining such a reckless, ridiculous proposal. It's even possible that there was a small part of me that was hesitating--a part of me that wanted to be talked out of it. He listened to everything I had to say, considered a while, and then opened his mouth to speak. What he said left me astonished. It was nothing less than the best advice he ever gave me: "...Go with your heart, son. It might not seem right. But if it feels right...do it."

The very last thing I expected was for my father to tell me to throw caution to the wind. If he had sprouted wings from his back and offered to fly me to Spain himself, I could hardly have been more surprised. It was so unlike the man I had known all through my childhood. The man who had silently withstood Jim Fontaine's stormy rages and scarcely put up a fight when his own marriage had fallen to pieces. I had never seen that side of him before. After that, there was no going back. I called Pat the following morning and said I was his man.

Three days later, on January 20th, 1982, I was on a flight from Manchester to Malaga, Spain. As we ascended into the clouds, I got a distinct feeling of rising above all the obstacles that I had spent my young life stumbling over. My head was swimming, and my limbs were flooded with a tingling sensation. I was practically vibrating with anticipation the entire flight, from takeoff to touchdown. The jolt of the plane's wheels hitting the runaway in Malaga couldn't compete with the turbulence I was experiencing internally. It seemed to me that my own body could barely contain my hunger for new experiences and my potential for artistic growth. Spain was my future, and my future was overflowing with surprises.

Little did I know that what was waiting for me at that sunny Spanish airport was the most extraordinary surprise that my life had ever dealt me.

CHAPTER 11:
THE GIRL AT THE AIRPORT

Not all those who wander are lost

— **J.R.R. Tolkien**

* * *

What was waiting for me was a 21-year-old woman named Anne Riley. When I cast my mind back to that day, I can't help but feel like fate must have had a hand in it all, somehow. The job offer from Pat O'Hare, the advice I got from my Dad, the wanderlust that I felt deep in my bones, the strange pull that Rumi wrote about centuries ago––all these seemingly random occurrences, and peculiar quirks of my character, and apparent strokes of good fortune conspired to put me on that plane. Something more than mere luck must have been at play, I'm sure of it. If I had been more content to stay put, or if Pat O'Hare had given the gig to someone else, if my Dad had cautioned me against pulling up my roots, I would have never had the chance to meet Anne Riley. I would have never met the woman who I married.

Anne Riley was just a girl at the time, but she would go on to become the most important person in my life. We had no way of knowing, back then, what fate had in store for us––and it would take some time for us to figure it out. It wasn't what you would call love at first sight. I was equal parts worn out and jet-lagged and bursting with excitement. Anne, from my point of view, was simply the first person who introduced herself to me after I disembarked the plane––the first of many people I would meet in Spain. What are the odds that the first person who extended their hand to me upon my arrival would be the person I was destined to spend the rest of my life with? I certainly thought she was attractive, and I was happy to see a friendly face and hear an English voice, but that's as far as my thinking went. If I'd somehow seen, in the moment I first held her hand, all the things we'd achieve and the adventures we'd go on, I would have dropped my luggage on the floor of the concourse and wept with joy. That chance meeting at the airport would change everything for the two of us.

But I was not hearing wedding bells ring, or fantasizing about building a family with her, as we exited the airport and got into the car the hotel had sent to fetch me. Like any first-time traveler in an unfamiliar country, I wanted nothing more than to take a shower, put on some clean clothes, and start getting my bearings. Anne gave me a little help with that latter point en route to the hotel, pointing out local landmarks and giving me a somewhat better sense of what to expect from this job that I had rushed into sight unseen. As we drove along, I remember feeling both nervous about the duties that would fall to me and the role I'd be taking on, and also eager to prove that Pat had been right to put his faith in me. I knew that I was there to play music and entertain the guests, but beyond that, I had no earthly idea what to expect. Of course, unbeknownst to me, the other occupant of the car was someone who would spend the next 40 years inspiring me, supporting me, strengthening my resolve, and keeping me sane. No one in history who has ever found himself heading into a daunting new job has ever had a better partner in their corner than the one I had.

When we arrived at the hotel, there were many other handshakes and introductions. More than I could hope to recall, looking back on it now—more than I could keep track of even at the time, I suspect. One of the men whose acquaintance I made that day was Joe Rubido, the hotel's general manager. Joe was a kind man who had a passion for music, and he seemed genuinely keen to see what I had to offer. Even in my somewhat discombobulated state, it was apparent to me that he wasn't just turning on the charm to help break the ice with the new hire.

Joe would go on to reconfirm that favorable first impression of him time and time again. He was hands down the best boss I ever had. What a man! And what a place! And what a wonderful moment in time!

The Hotel Belplaya was a beautiful resort located on the coast of Torremolinos in the Costa del Sol. It was a glamorous establishment, but approachable at the same time. Inviting rather than imposing, and without a hint of snobbishness. Our clientele consisted mainly of holidaymakers from Britain, Germany, and the Netherlands, all of whom were descending upon the hotel with the common goal of soaking up the sun and enjoying the breathtaking vistas of southern Spain. As part of the hotel's entertainment team, I was tasked with keeping its guests busy and contented throughout the week. My teammates and I organized a range of activities, ranging from exercise classes, to bingo, to pool games, to late-night disco.

Hotel Belplaya

The activities that were of most interest to me, I'm sure I don't need to tell you, were the nightly live concerts. I was the leader of the Belplaya's five-piece band. We performed every night, and I loved every minute of it.

As you can imagine, the ensuing days and weeks proved to be a bit of a blur. When I wasn't learning the ropes, I was finding myself dazzled by the exotic sights and sounds swirling around me. But the details of that first night are branded on my memory, set apart from all the hubbub that followed. After settling in, I rendezvoused with Anne in the hotel lounge, where we talked about music and sat by the piano. I doubt we could have possibly been all alone in there, but I'll be damned if I can remember a single other soul being in the room. I played a few of my favorite songs for her, including one or two by Barry Manilow, who was one of her favorite artists. I could tell that she and I shared a love for music. That, in the beginning, was enough to forge an instant connection between us. As I played and sang for Anne, I could feel her favorite song, Manilow's "Lonely Together," becoming one of my favorites too. I can see now that this moment supplied the seed that would, in time, grow into the relationship we have today. It would be another year before we started to fall in love, but that night was the catalyst. The start of something that would reinvent us both, and make us happier than we'd ever imagined.

It truly is impossible to put into words what Anne means to me. I'm going to make a game effort, regardless, despite knowing damn well that I'm doomed to come up short. I will inevitably fail to convey to you the depths of the love I feel for her––every page of this book, from this point on, will be a heartsick chronicle of that failure. She and I have been through exhilarating highs and terrifying lows together, but the good times and the bad times alike have done nothing to shake our belief that the bond we have is exceedingly unique and special. At the time of writing this book, we have been together for four decades, and things are better than ever. It's not always been great. There have been indiscretions that have threatened to break us apart forever, and I am ashamed to say that I am responsible for all of them. Of all the things in life I am grateful for, the mere fact that Anne is by my side is the one I cherish most.

I try to put myself in the shoes of that jet-lagged boy sitting on the piano bench beside her, that first night in Spain, and I find that I can't. Not completely. The love I harbor today, 40 years on, keeps distorting my perception and crowding into my memories. It's like looking at the past through a window streaked with rain. You can never get a clear view—but it's enchanting all the same. I imagine myself sneaking glances at her as a young man and thinking, as if through some form of time travel, all of the same happy, love-struck thoughts that cross my mind whenever I look at her now.

CHAPTER 12:
WHERE'S YOUR BALL?

The only way to do great work is to love what you do
—Steve Jobs

* * *

The Belplaya was an endlessly stimulating environment, one that lent itself well to both work and play. The line between the two was pretty smudgy at the best of times, as my playmates were also my coworkers. I learned so much from all of them. Joe Rubido, in particular, was a strong influence. He was a schmoozer for sure--he had a special knack for endearing himself to people. There was no tense situation that he couldn't defuse by cracking a joke and flashing a smile. I watched him smooth down a lot of ruffled feathers in the three years I spent working at his hotel. He was a quintessential Spaniard, save for one strange detail: a cockney accent that he had picked up during his time in the UK. What a brilliant personality he was. A legend. It was Joe who taught me the importance of staying positive, and showed me the power it can have in influencing your relationships. He was unfailingly outgoing and friendly, though he was also capable of turning on a dime and putting his foot down when something wasn't to his liking. A place like the Belplaya can't run on jokes and smiles alone--not even Joe's jokes and smiles.

After Anne, Joe is the figure from that period of my life who looms largest in my memory. But I met so many fantastic people in that hotel. Brian Mundell was another. He was the Belplaya's entertainment manager and a key player in its main shows. You'll never meet a more lively or versatile performer.

He did an Elvis Presley tribute, a Neil Diamond tribute, and even a hypnosis show, with Anne and I providing the backing vocals. Anne was more of an asset to these acts than she gave herself credit for. I was always impressed with her vocal talents, but she had zero confidence and seemingly had no desire to ever step out on her own. Well, you know me—I wasn't going to stand for that.

One morning, I decided to take matters into my own hands. I added Anne to the roster for that night's variety show without telling her. When she woke up and saw her name and photo on the poster advertising the show, she was more than mortified. Closer to petrified. As I recall she spent the better part of that day in the bathroom, feeling sick to her stomach and stressed out beyond belief. But when the time came for her to perform, she absolutely killed it, as I knew she would. It was a gamble, on my part, thrusting her into the spotlight like that. But it went so well that there weren't any hard feelings afterward. And I didn't see her as a potential romantic partner at that time, outside of the occasional stray flirty remark, so it didn't strike me as an unreasonable stunt to pull. She and I were mates, and one of the marks of a good mate is that they can take a prank at their expense—and then get you back when you least expect it.

Maybe it's wrong of me to refer to it as a prank, though. After all, it's not as though I was trying to humiliate her. I knew that she would be sensational. Watching her step out of her comfort zone and conquer her fears was amazing. I don't think she ever fully gained the confidence that her talent warranted—at least, not during our days at the Belplaya—but for my money she's the single best entertainer I've ever shared the spotlight with. She can get an audience in the palm of her hands and keep them there, night after night after night. It's a remarkable thing to witness.

In my second or third year at the Belplaya, when I was about twenty-two, a new guitarist named Sean McMenemy took the place by storm. In no time at all we found ourselves wondering how we had ever gotten along without him. Sean was a lad a few years younger than me, with curly ginger hair and an infectious sense of fun. His father was Lawrie McMenemy, the football manager for Southampton, and one of the most well-known and well-regarded football managers in the history of the game. Joe Rubido had a number of connections in the British sports world and had a working relationship with Lawrie, which is how Sean came to join our merry band. He and I hit it off immediately. At that time the hotel's band consisted of me and a bunch of Spanish musicians. So when Joe approached me and said that a talented young bloke from back home would soon be joining our ensemble, I was delighted. All of us got on famously with Sean. Had it not been for Sean showing up, I doubt we ever would have hit upon the idea for "Where's Your Ball?"

Now, this requires some context. For a member of the Belplaya's entertainment team, which only consisted of six people, the workday was long and jam-packed. Exercise classes started at 9 a.m., and late night disco ended at 3 a.m. And the six of us were busting our asses to keep the guests entertained that entire time. It was mad. Were it not for the strong camaraderie I shared with Anne, Sean, and the others, it would have been too grueling to be worthwhile in the long run. If you have to work punishing shifts day in and day out, take my advice, and try to do it with your best friends––and better yet, try to do it someplace where the weather is as nice as it is in the Costa del Sol. Unsurprisingly, we tended to wrap up our workdays in a fairly delirious state of mind. After a few weeks of that kind of delirium, some curious ideas start to take hold. We had to invent all sorts of wacky games to play between ourselves to stay sane and motivated––none wackier than "Where's Your Ball?" I couldn't tell you which one of us came up with the rules. We picked up six foam Nerf balls from a toy store and it was decided that each of us would have to conceal their ball somewhere on their person at all times.

All that summer, the cries of "Where's your ball!?" rang out in the barrooms and on the beaches. If someone asked you to produce your ball, and you couldn't, you had to contribute 100 pesetas to the end-of-season party. It was less a game for us than a newfound religion. These sorts of high jinks, naturally, are always funnier when you approach them with the utmost seriousness. In the first week, no one remembered their ball, and the pile of pesetas started to grow at a rather worrying rate. We learned pretty quickly that it was best to carry our ball with us wherever we went––no matter how much awkwardness this created.

The six of us were always innovating and trying to think up ways to trap and outwit one another. One time, I was refereeing a game of water polo, clad in nothing but a Speedo, when I suddenly heard the shrill sound of a whistle pierce the air. I turned to see Anne standing beside the pool with a look of triumph on her face. She spat the whistle out of her mouth and shouted: "Terry! Where's your ball?" Without missing a beat, I reached into the front of my Speedo and pulled out a pristine yellow Nerf ball, much to Anne's consternation.

Anne had no intention of taking that defeat lying down, as I would soon learn. All she had to do was lie in wait until I was even more vulnerable (and wearing even less clothing) than I had been that day in the pool. She knew that she wouldn't have to bide her time for very long. I like to say that our experience at the Hotel Belplaya was the classic triptych of sex, drugs, and rock 'n roll––but without the drugs (save for the booze, and the endless supply of Spanish sunshine, which was intoxicating in its own right). All of us had our fair share of indiscretions with the hotel's guests. The atmosphere in which these conquests took place was one of freewheeling liberation. There wasn't a drop of negativity to be found. We were all just kids having fun, carousing, and messing about with balls, as kids are often do. Still, that was no excuse to drop one's guard––and I didn't, not even the one time Anne thought for sure she'd gotten the better of me.

A large group of golfers booked a stay at the hotel, the summer that Sean came aboard, the summer that all of our madcap chicanery was in full swing. I ended up having a short, casual fling with a married woman from this golfing group. That in and of itself might have been a mistake, depending on your values––but, in my view, the far greater mistake was my telling Anne and Brian that she and I were retiring to her room so that they could let us know if the rest of the golfing party came back to the hotel. How foolish I was to think the two of them would have my best interests at heart.

No sooner had this lovely woman and I leapt into bed together than I heard a knock at the door, followed immediately by the alarming sound of the door swinging wide open. Panic set in, and my mind raced. Had the other golfers returned? Why hadn't my two loyal lookouts warned me? When I saw Anne and Brian enter the room, pushing a vacuum cleaner along in front of them, I had my answer. "Housekeeping," they both cried out tauntingly. "Housekeeping! Where's your ball?"

I hesitated only long enough to cast a sheepish, apologetic glance at the bed's other occupant before reaching beneath the sheets and producing the ball in question. The poor woman, god bless her, had no idea what was going on.

I can't say that I'm proud of everything we got up to during our days at that hotel. But it was a time of freedom, frivolity, and discovery. A period in my life that I'm sure I'll never forget. And for what it's worth, to this day I don't know if I've ever seen Anne or Brian laugh harder than they did when they saw that ball come out from under the blanket.

CHAPTER 13:
LONELY TOGETHER

The greatest thing you'll ever learn is just to love and be loved in return
—Nat King Cole

* * *

I was in Spain for three wonderful years in total. It flew by much too quickly, but there was no helping that. There was so much work to be done and so much fun to be had. I don't know how our little crew of entertainers was able to pull it off. My RAF training came in handy on more than one occasion. There's even a case to be made that I excelled at "Where's Your Ball" because I'd been through basic training and my fellow players had not. Let's just say that when the time came to throw the end-of-season party, I was not its number one financier.

As spectacular as the Belplaya was, I'm happy to say that our lives were not entirely confined to it. Outside of the hotel, just past the main entrance, if you turned right, there was a promenade to walk down, with a wide sidewalk flanked by pubs and eateries and small shops selling t-shirts and souvenir trinkets. Once you got past the more tourist-friendly areas, there was a wealth of new things to discover. We'd go out all the time, Anne and I and the others. You had to decompress and get away from the hotel's dizzying atmosphere, even if it meant burning the candle at both ends. Sometimes after the show at night, we'd be too wired to sleep and not ready for the next day to begin. We'd go out together, as a group or as a twosome, and drink sangria, eat paella, and watch the sunrise. There was a Swedish restaurant called Estocolmo we loved to go to where they served meat on these large wooden blocks. That was our favorite place to eat in the Costa del Sol. The fact that I had to travel all the way to Spain to discover Swedish cuisine ought to give you some idea of how much variety there was to be found there.

My brother David got in on the action eventually, joining the entertainment team after I'd been at the Belplaya long enough to put in a good word for him. I love David dearly. He's one of the funniest people I know, even with that wicked short temper of his. As soon as he stepped off the plane he was struck speechless by the first ray of Spanish sunshine that fell over him, just as I had been when I'd first arrived.

In Manchester, it rains three hundred days a year. That's just a fact of life there, as basic as gravity. I can't speak for David, but I decided, the instant I felt that tropical warmth on my face, that I couldn't picture myself going back to those drizzly skies and those streets dotted with puddles. I didn't think there was a way for me to remain in Spain forever, but wherever I went next, I wanted it to be warm. And, increasingly, as time went on, I found that I had another wish. Wherever I wound up, I wanted Anne to be there with me.

Have you ever had the sense that something was meant to be? Not in retrospect, but in the heat of the moment? As I look back over this period of my life, it all feels fated to me. My life, as it exists today, strikes me as a foregone conclusion. But that's hindsight talking. The first time that I can remember that feeling settling over me in real time was the day I took Anne to Tivoli World.

She and I had a really strong, purely platonic friendship. For the first year in Spain, Anne was in a relationship with the DJ in Spain called Paul and we were both living life to the fullest. She would even set me up with her girlfriends from time to time, and we always had a good laugh about it afterward. Out of everyone at the Belplaya (and everyone I had known in England, for that matter), she was far and away my closest friend. There was a rapport between us that was never forced and never rang false. When she quit and moved back to the UK, it was the first serious blow that my happiness had sustained since I had found myself in Spain. We kept in touch, writing letters back and forth to one another frequently. Long letters in which we wore our hearts on our sleeve, but never made any romantic overtures. We truly were best friends. Our level of intimacy was deep enough to grant me insight into all aspects of her life, including her relationship woes. She was nearing the end of her relationship with Paul as it was no longer working out. My romantic rendezvouses in Spain were nothing serious, by and large--perhaps because, whether I realized it or not, my heart was already spoken for.

We were fifteen months into this funny friendship of ours, still carrying on this platonic correspondence, when I coaxed her into returning to the Belplaya--just for a couple of weeks. I needed someone to fill in for the current girl we had on the entertainment team. After some deliberation, she said yes, and within days she was on a plane back to Malaga.

During those two weeks things started to crystallize for me, beginning on an unconscious level. The Belplaya was the sort of place that could make years of your life go past in the blink of an eye. A couple of weeks was nothing. So I knew we had to wring as much enjoyment from it as we possibly could. Doing so came naturally to us.

We were having a blast, Anne and I, back under the Belplaya's roof. It was just like old times--until, suddenly, wonderfully, it wasn't. One day, on a morning just like any other, I woke up and walked downstairs to grab breakfast. Anne was behind the front desk, going over the excursions for the day. I was completely sober, but something must have been addling my mind. Maybe I'd awoken in some sort of trance--maybe I'd been dreaming about her. I'll never know what possessed me. All

I can tell you is that I walked straight up to the desk, locked eyes with her, and said "I'm gonna marry you one day." And with that, I walked off. She looked perplexed, called me a "weirdo," and we both burst out laughing. It was not premeditated, and I haven't got a clue where it came from––but it turned out to be a damn good prediction. Anne was also right, of course. It was weirdo behavior on my part.

That day, we went on an excursion to Tivoli World with some of the hotel's guests. Tivoli World is a theme park located in Benalmádena on the Costa del Sol. It's a grand place, boasting a range of rides and recreation options, including a wooden roller coaster, a Ferris wheel, and various water-based attractions. All of these diversions, however, paled in comparison to its gardens, which are a real feast for the eyes. Once the guests we were supervising had dispersed into the park, that's where Anne and I found ourselves. It was probably the quietest corner of Tivoli World, and certainly the prettiest. We walked for a long time past lines of colorful flowers and tropical plants, listening to the distant sounds of delighted screams wafting over from the rest of the park. We were still on the clock, but chaperoning adult holidaymakers on an outing isn't like shepherding schoolkids on a class field trip. They were content to enjoy the park on their own, and we were happy to get a little time to ourselves. In that moment, we were just like any other two patrons of Tivoli World. All our obligations and our other entanglements dropped away as we walked.

Without premeditation, I took Anne's hand in mine. I know it must have felt strange to her, but it felt right to me. Profoundly right. And the strangeness of it must not have been enough to scare her off, because––to my momentary surprise and my everlasting happiness––she didn't take her hand away. She held on tight and did not let go. Neither did I. In a sense, we never did.

And that was it. We crossed a line together, that day at Tivoli World, and away we went. We walked into those gardens as friends and walked out of them as lovers. We fell completely and unashamedly in love.

Fate stepped in. There's no other explanation that I can see. The joy I felt, interlacing my fingers with hers, eclipsed all the other pleasures I'd known up to that point in my life. I became conscious of a love that existed between us that was not some abstract concept, but had the substance and solidity of something real. It was like the first time I held a record with my own songs on it in my hands. Somehow this intangible thing had taken shape in front of me, and I could touch it. That's how it feels to love Anne Riley. It was meant to be. I could feel it that day in the gardens, and I can still feel it now. I adore her to this day.

CHAPTER 14:
CALIFORNIA DREAMIN'

Here you leave today and enter the world of yesterday,
tomorrow, and fantasy — **Walt Disney**

* * *

I don't want my focus on my relationship with Anne, life-changing as it was, to distract me too much from the many friendships I formed during this time period. I knew a ton of fantastic people at the Belplaya, including a few who I've yet to mention by name, and they all impacted my life in ways both large and small. My brother David, Sean McMenemy, Tony and Hedy Foreman, Brian and Sue Mundell, Joe Rubido, Jose Maria Del Olmo—the list could go on. Even though most of us were thousands of miles away from home, we formed our own tight-knit family and made countless memories that we'll be laughing about for the rest of our lives.

My friendship with Sean, in particular, was a source of endless amusement, as well as being eye-opening in certain ways. Despite the distaste I'd acquired in my adulthood for Manchester's dreary weather, I was, and will always remain, a dyed-in-the-wool football fan. Sean knew this. It was one of the many subjects we bonded over. Whenever I found myself back in the UK, over the coming years, I'd make a point of dropping in on him. I would often stay at his house, where I met his father, Lawrie. Once I even got the chance to have dinner with his Dad and Michael Parkinson, an experience that left me totally starry-eyed.

I told Sean that I was making arrangements to fly to America, for the first time in my life, to visit some family members I'd not seen in years. My mother and her new husband had emigrated to the US some time after she divorced my father. Relocating across the Atlantic, in those days, was not a trivial undertaking. You were putting a lot of distance between yourself and whatever loved ones you left behind, creating a gap that could only be bridged by the occasional letter or long-distance phone call, not by FaceTime, or any of the other marvelous gadgets we have at our fingertips nowadays. But then, the circumstances of my parents' divorce had already torn a ragged rift down the middle of my family. All that my mother's emigration did was make it literal and lend it geographical dimensions. She had taken most of the kids with her when she left. I had siblings in the US who I hadn't seen in ages––and a couple who I'd never met at all. It was high time that I remedied that.

I asked Sean to tag along on this trip, and he unhesitatingly agreed. I must have made some effort to brief him on the basics of all the family drama so that he'd have an idea of what he was getting himself into. But I'm sure nothing I could have said would have deterred him. He and I flew to California, where my mother's family lived, and the two of us had a fantastic couple of weeks there. It was a monumental experience. The size of everything was staggering. We stepped off the plane, and I was instantly blown away by the glamour of the Golden State. I have a story that I still like to tell onstage, one I've been getting mileage out of for years now, about the moment of culture shock that rattled me the most, when I first set foot on American soil. It's a bit embarrassing to admit, but the thing that made the deepest impression on me, our first night in California, was laying eyes on an Arby's for the first time. That gigantic neon sign just knocked me sideways.

Big and bright as its sign might have been, however, in terms of sheer magnificence, Arby's had nothing on Disneyland. I'm sure any American would cosign that statement. I honestly got choked up as I walked through the gates of that iconic theme park. For a poor kid from Openshaw, getting to spend a day in Disneyland felt like some kind of wondrous waking dream. The colorful rides, the catchy music, and the larger-than-life characters made my eyes well up with tears. I must have been in a somewhat emotionally vulnerable and childlike state of mind, that day, given that I'd come to California to reconnect with my mother. Wherever that surge of emotion came from had to have been somewhere deep inside me. I've still got a box of pictures, somewhere or another, that Sean and I snapped that day. It was a genuinely magical experience.

But the highlight of our stay was catching up with my Mum and my brothers and sisters. I got to meet my two youngest siblings, Jamie-Lee and Wesley, for the very first time. I'm twenty-three years older than the two of them, but we bonded instantly. My mother seemed content to me, and thrilled to have so many of us in one place again. It made me happy to see her get the chance to reestablish herself somewhere far away from all the chaos that her divorce and remarriage had caused.

Eric, the man she had married, as you'll recall, was my cousin on my Dad's side. His mother was my Dad's sister. The strain that scandal put on my extended family was significant. Those were some very tough years for many of my relatives. I had already left home by then, so it didn't impact me all that much. I was able to throw myself into the rigors of basic training, and then the hectic life of a musician. That's how I kept myself occupied and tuned out the worst of the familial infighting. My younger siblings weren't so lucky. David, in particular, took the whole thing hard. When Eric and my mother moved to the US, they took with them the three youngest kids who were alive at the time, my siblings Wendy, Andrew, and Peter. Susan, the second eldest of us, followed them out there not long after. David and I, however, stayed behind in the UK. Because he was younger than I was, and less independent at the time of the divorce, David felt rejected, and he continued to struggle with these feelings of rejection for a long time. I don't think he ever truly reconciled with our Mum, or made peace with himself.

Sean and I spent two weeks in California before flying back to Spain. Suddenly those hotel hallways I knew so well began to lose some of the luster. It wasn't long before I started to find myself pining for the wide open spaces of the US again––and it wasn't just the allure of round-the-clock fast food that called to me, mind you. I had felt that strange pull again, during my stay there. The same one that had urged me to take Pat O'Hare up on the offer that had led me to Spain in the first place. It seemed to me that there was so much room to grow in America. So many new things to see and do. Despite being bathed in the heavenly sunlight of the Costa del Sol, I kept catching myself fantasizing about the San Fernando Valley, where my Mum had settled down, and about all the places that lay beyond it, places steeped in opportunity and potential, places that were still waiting to be discovered.

I pitched Anne on the idea of moving to California with me and starting our life together there. She would have been well within her rights to laugh, call me a "weirdo" again, and leave it at that. But she didn't. She not only heard me out but actually seemed to think the proposal had some merit. Before long, we were both hooked on the idea and after that, the outcome was assured. We gave our notice to Joe Rubido and said goodbye to the place that had brought the two of us together. A place, as well as a time, that will forever reside in the warmest part of our hearts––as warm as a sandy Spanish beach at the height of summer.

I'm fortunate enough to still be in contact with many of the friends we made back then, thanks to the world of online social media. I like to think that if I were to bump into any of them tomorrow on the street, we could pick up right where we left off, and stay out all night long, eating paella, drinking sangria, telling jokes, and singing songs. And maybe in the middle of all this, one of them would turn to me, quite suddenly, and say, in a serious tone of voice, but with a spark of mischief in their eyes: "Terry––where's your ball?" I wouldn't have it on me, I'm sorry to say. I lost that years ago.

CHAPTER 15:
THE CRESTING WAVE

The sea is dangerous and its storms terrible, but these obstacles have never been sufficient reason to remain ashore —**Ferdinand Magellan**

* * *

At some point before leaving Spain, Anne and I bought a car. An old white VW buggy--a love bug. It was a piece of shit, but it got us from place to place. We liked having our own set of wheels, Anne and I. We picked up duo gigs here and there, for a time, in a string of bars that would have been nothing to write home about, had they been anywhere other than the coast of Spain. Playing together, just the two of us, was great fun, and rather unlike our experience of performing for the tourists that steadily streamed through the Belplaya. You never knew what sort of crowd you were going to get, but that uncertainty helped us to refine our act. The edge of the stage is a line separating what you can control from what you can't control--one of your jobs, as a musician, is to stay on top of everything that's happening on your side of that line. Slowly but surely, Anne and I perfected our patter and stage presence. This extra practice would give us a leg up when we finally made it stateside. But first, we had a voyage ahead of us.

When she and I made up our minds to hit the trail for good and move to America, we hatched a plan that entailed driving our beat-up VW all the way to the UK. We looked at that junker of ours, said a prayer, loaded it up, and took off. The Belplaya is on the southern coast of Spain, and we had to make it all the way up through Granada and Madrid to Santander on the northern coast, in order to catch a car ferry to Southampton. What we did not know, when we settled on this scheme of ours, was that the Bay of Biscay is notorious for being one of the roughest seas in the world. Years and years later, Anne and I would find ourselves performing regularly on cruise ships. This is something that we've taken great pleasure in doing right up to the present. I've now spent countless hours out on the open ocean, and I've gained an appreciation for both its awesome majesty and its terrible power. But as a pair of landlubbers in their early twenties, we had no idea what we were getting ourselves into. These days, Anne and I are constantly crossing paths with people on our cruises who will go to great lengths to avoid any itineraries that include the Bay of Biscay. It's that rough––and that dangerous. Ignorant of all this, Anne and I arrived on Spain's northern coast in the dead of night and slept in our car, waiting for dawn and for the ferry that would take us back to England. Had we known what sort of crossing the Bay of Biscay had in store for us, we would not have slept as soundly as we did.

The ferry was actually supposed to leave that same night, but it was delayed on account of bad weather. I now know that this was a terrifically bad omen. If the weather in the Bay of Biscay is regarded as being so bad as to make traversal impossible, even by the local seafarers, that means the weather is very, *very* bad indeed. At its best, it's dreadful. If it was too choppy to sail in, it must have been downright lethal. That should have been a warning sign––but there's a good chance that, even if Anne and I had recognized it as such, and even if we'd been savvier with regards to the sea, we still wouldn't have heeded it. We were young and headstrong. And if we'd been afraid of making mistakes and taking chances, we never would have left Spain to begin with. We spent the night in our car and figured that would probably be the height of our discomfort for the duration of our trip back to the UK. How wrong we were.

We drove onto the ferry the following morning, parked alongside a few large trucks, and chained our wheels down. All the automobiles were arranged in tight rows, packed in close together. After days on the road and a long night of fitful sleep behind the wheel, we were eager to crawl out of the love bug and into a bunk bed. The ferry wasn't the height of luxury, especially compared to the Belplaya hotel we'd called home for years, but we each had a mattress to collapse onto, and there was a little cafe area, so we reasoned we'd at least get the chance to put our feet up and relax awhile. I can't remember now if the ferry was advertised as taking twenty-four hours or if we signed on for a twelve-hour trip that wound up taking twice as long. Whatever the case may be, we were at sea for a full day––and it was, without question, one of the most thoroughly miserable days of my entire life.

Anne and I were put in a small cabin with two truck drivers we'd never met before. Ten feet by sixteen feet, at the most. Four beds and one toilet. More than once, in the course of the ordeal that ensued, I found myself wishing that this arrangement could somehow be reversed––that we could instead be given four toilets and one bed. It's not as though any of us were able to get much sleep. Minute after minute, for hours upon hours, the car ferry plowed into one colossal wave after another. For a full day, we were tossed like a bath toy on a series of twenty-five to thirty-foot waves that turned our stomachs inside out and, frankly, made us fear for our lives. Anne and I had never sailed and were blissfully unaware of what the ocean was capable of. At first, she and I sized up the situation with our usual optimism. "Well," we said to one another, "this isn't so bad. It's a bit bumpy." That was before the waves swelled to their full height and really started hammering us. The two truckers, who you might assume were made of stronger stuff than we were, did not fare any better than we did. The four of us quickly fell into a rotation. The toilet was never not in use. Anne and I, and these two poor souls we'd just met, spent a day of our lives running back and forth from the bathroom, taking turns throwing up. It was, in a word, horrifying. There were times when I genuinely thought that Anne and I were going to die in that cramped cabin alongside those two seasick strangers, with the lion's share of our life's journey still ahead of us.

If you've never ridden a wave of that size, you can't imagine how nerve-wracking and stomach-churning it is. There was a certain awful rhythm to it––something that Anne and I, as musicians, were eventually able to recognize, though it took us a while to wrap our heads around what was actually happening. We'd go up, and then the vessel would level out, and we'd think, *oh, thank god, the wave's come and gone.* But our relief was reliably premature. We hadn't made it over the wave––we were only riding the crest of it. And then we'd find ourselves in a sudden, sickening descent. Down, down, down, and then *boom*––a deafening crash, as we smashed into the surface of the ocean, with such force that we felt sure we'd go under and sink like a stone. This went on for twenty-four interminable hours. It would take a king's ransom to get me to sail the waters of the Bay of Biscay nowadays, even on a modern cruise ship with massive stabilizers, which this sea-tossed Spanish car ferry assuredly did not have. We made landfall in Southampton and staggered, still nauseous, with ashen faces and legs made of jelly and made our way below deck to our car––only to find it standing practically alone in a field of wreckage. Numerous cars parked alongside it had been smashed flat under the trucks, which had come loose from their chains during one or more of those terrifying 30 foot ascents and descents. Our buggy might have been a junker, but we were able to drive off in it, and there were many other passengers who could not say the same. We disembarked in Southampton with no appetite, but with a functional vehicle (which we ultimately bequeathed to Anne's dad, before we left for America). The important thing is that we were still alive, and that we'd made it. We were grateful for that. That was one of the worst storms Anne and I have weathered together. But it would not be the last. Gratitude has gotten us through all of them.

CHAPTER 16:
LOOKING FORWARD

Family, whether by blood or inheritance, is meant to be our sanctuary.
Yet, all too often, it's where we encounter our deepest heartaches
—Iyanla Vanzant

* * *

It was around this time that Anne and I embarked on a fateful journey––not to the United States, but to visit her family in Liverpool. After our perilous crossing, it didn't strike either of us as a very ambitious expedition, but that was all to the good. And in terms of the thoughts and feelings it inspired, and the friendships it fostered, it was almost as much of an odyssey as our trip to Southampton had been. In 1984, the Rileys were one of many typical scouse families dwelling in the heart of Bootle. That part of Liverpool had been heavily impacted by the decline of the docks and the loss of local industries in years prior. Unemployment was high, and crime rates were likewise elevated. By the mid-1980s, Bootle was generally regarded as a tough place to grow up––a tough place to call home. The people of Bootle were equal to these challenges, however. I was struck by the resilience they displayed in the face of all the difficulties that had sprung up in their community. They were terrific people across the board––tough enough to get along in a hostile environment, but not so tough as to lose their kindness and neighborliness. Bootle was an easy community to love for all its problems. Everyone looked out for one another, and families frequently banded together to support one another through hard times.

I met most of Anne's brothers and sisters on this first visit. Anne is the eldest of eight, so there were quite a few new names and faces for me to keep straight. I was eager to make a good impression and not get any of them mixed up. The Rileys were a close-knit clan, and in that way, they represented Bootle in a microcosm. I knew that the best way to win them over would be to match their friendliness and sincerity. It's a time-honored truth that, after you've successfully courted the love of your life, the next task that falls to you is to do what you can to court the rest of their family.

Fortunately, I learned straight away that I didn't have to put on any sort of elaborate performance when I was around Anne's people. One of my many strokes of luck in winding up with her was marrying into a family that, by and large, seems to like me for who I really am. I haven't ever had to do much more than be myself. We all took a trip to a small theme park in Southport called Pleasureland and had a great time together. That was the bonding experience that first assured me that I was going to be welcomed into the Riley clan.

I don't mean to suggest that there were no hiccups, however. I've since gone on to have some interesting relationships over the years with Anne's brothers and sisters, not all of which have been perfectly rosy. But the best of the friendships I gained from meeting Anne's siblings was more than worth the occasional headaches that came with becoming an honorary Riley. Anne's youngest brother, Ste, has been my closest friend for over 30 years now. He's a brilliant person, about whom I'll have much more to say in a short while. The only major strike against him that I can see is his unconscionable love for Liverpool Football Club--I could never understand, much less condone, such a terrible lack of judgment!

The most valuable thing I got from that trip, though, was not newfound friendship, but rather a deeper degree of insight into the woman that I loved. I saw a lot of Anne in Bootle and a lot of Bootle in Anne. I had no difficulty tracing her tenacity, her cleverness, her generosity, and her resourcefulness back to the neck of the woods where she'd been raised. I was consumed with a complicated mix of excitement and uncertainty around this time. The big move to America was looming on the horizon. I knew there was a good chance that Anne and I wouldn't land on our feet immediately and that she and I likely had some lean months ahead of us. Getting to see the stock that she came from, and what they were capable of, gave me incredible peace of mind. I left Liverpool feeling more confident than ever that Anne was up for whatever adversities the US could lob at us. Her strength would buoy my own, and together we would find a way to make it work. The day in Pleasureland had also been affirming in a different way--ever since that trip to Tivoli World that changed my life, theme parks have always reminded me of Anne, mentally transporting me back to the night it all began.

Anne has one sister who I've feuded with off and on over the years and who has consistently sought to sow discord in the family. One of the surest signs of my good fortune is that I've found it incredibly easy, for the most part, to maintain a sunny attitude, as I've looked back over my life in the process of writing this book. I'm pleased to say that I don't have very many enemies. But there are individuals who I've butted heads with in my lifetime, and one or two of them have had the surname Riley. Still, on the whole, I consider it a privilege to be counted as one of them. Coming to know your in-laws requires you to take on the burden of a lot of history that you weren't around for, and contend with grievances that you're ill-equipped to understand. My own family was fractured, by the time I met Anne––it couldn't have been easy for her, having to get acquainted with people on both sides of that divide, on both sides of the ocean.

As a matter of fact, my family's situation was, if anything, a bit more fraught than I've let on, up to this point. My mother remarried first, but my father was not far behind. He remained unmarried for roughly a year and a half to two years, before proposing to a woman he worked with. For over 20 years, my Dad's day job was crafting paintbrushes at Mosley Stone Brushmakers in Stockport. While he pursued music at night, his days were dedicated to making brushes. It was here that he met his second wife, Jean. The two of them hadn't had any sort of relationship when he and my mother were still together, but after the divorce, needless to say, all bets were off. From where I was standing, it seemed as though they just fell into it. There was an element of happenstance to the arrangement. David and I––the two kids who remained in the UK––worked hard to foster a close relationship with her, and she made that unnecessarily difficult for us. This is another area where my cheerful disposition starts to falter somewhat. I can honestly say that David and I, along with the rest of our siblings, would have welcomed our stepmother with open arms had she actually permitted us to do so. David, in particular, being younger, would have benefited hugely if he'd felt that his family had been made whole again. But she was not interested in being all that friendly with us, much less maternally affectionate.

If I had to guess—and, given the distance she created, guesses are my only option—I would say that this hostility was born of insecurity. A woman in her position might have felt that she was competing with her predecessor, and some of that resentment must have spilled over to her predecessor's offspring. She seemingly never had much use for us. It was a pattern of behavior with her that persisted for years. I needn't tell you that my Dad did not resist it as much as I would've liked. He literally had to sneak behind her back and tell lies in order to visit his kids in the USA, rather than simply stand his ground. I can only hope that she made him happy in their private life, separate from the rest of us—which was the way she wanted it. We tolerated our stepmom for my father's sake. Sometimes toleration is the only thing a person has coming to them, the only thing they have a right to expect. When my Dad passed away, we were in Norway at the time, and Nick and I flew to be at the funeral. The treatment we received from my Dad's wife and her 2 daughters, Jill and Diane, was despicable. As they say, the apple does not fall far from the tree. Not only were we pretty much ignored and shunned at the funeral, but I learned that it took them less than 24 hours to "adjust" my Dad's will to remove his children from any benefits when his wife died. They also refused to give me any rights to his ashes or even tell me where they were. To this day, I still do not know where my Dad's ashes are being kept.

I thought about my own family a fair deal, during that first trip to Liverpool. Anne and I were on the verge of starting a new life together—the verge, perhaps, of starting a family together, before too much longer. I think I wanted some assurance that whatever family we created together would be happier, and more intact, than mine. That's always the goal when you have children—to improve on what came before while not losing sight of all the good things you inherited from your own parents. Parenthood was still a long way off for Anne and me in 1984, but we had no way of knowing that. America was just around the corner, and it seemed to us that, once we got there, anything might happen.

This was not a bad guess, as it turned out. We had no idea how right we were.

CHAPTER 17:
STATESIDE

Music is the soundtrack of your life
—Dick Clark

* * *

In early 1985, Anne and I moved to California, where we immediately set about looking for gigs as a duo once again, the same way we'd done in Spain, to supplement our
hotel work. It was the sort of life that appealed to us, the sort of life we understood.
We'd played in a number of crummy venues for lousy pay in various towns along the
Spanish coast—and while the jobs themselves had not been glamorous, the glamour
of the setting had gone a long way towards making up for that, in our minds. But not
all the venues were crummy. Anne and I performed at a live music bar and restaurant
called Intermezzo. This was different to some of the smaller, run-down places we
performed. The Intermezzo was a class joint situated between Marbella and Puerto
Banus. We had a blast in that venue!

The first several weeks of chasing down gigs in the US were a lot like that.
California may not be as exotic as Spain's southern coast, all things being equal. But
to our eyes, in the mid-1980s, it very nearly was. We're talking about a time and a
place, remember, where music and movies were thriving. Being in the midst of all
that activity, and all that creativity, was totally enthralling for us.

We fell head over heels for America. It called to us, and so we answered. My
Mum and most of my siblings were over here. Anne and I weren't teenagers anymore,
we were in our early twenties. It all just made perfect sense. We interlaced our fingers,
like we had that day in Tivoli Gardens, and took the plunge. *This is it*, we thought.
Let's give it a go.

We stayed at my mother's place in the San Fernando Valley for a while. I didn't
like to impose on her, but really, it couldn't have been much of an imposition—we
had virtually no possessions, and so we took up very little space. We certainly had

no musical equipment. All we had was a bit of money. Just enough to buy some basic gear, so that we wouldn't be laughed out of any auditions we went into. Enough to get started.

Anne got herself part-time job as a server at a Sizzler steak restaurant in Granada Hills and I found myself selling organs and keyboards at Organtown - a music store in West Covina mall. I spent at least 3 hours a day driving from Granada hills to that mall for work, but I didn't care....we were living our dream in America! We started lining up gigs, in spite of our lousy gear. There was a joint in Northridge called The Strawberry Patch that used to pay us 50 bucks a night, three nights a week. The pay itself was crap, but we were happy to be working--particularly after we became aware of that peculiar American custom known as "tipping." Most nights, with a little crowd work, we were able to triple or quadruple our earnings, thanks to the alcohol-fueled generosity of our audience. We gained experience, and cultivated a small following, and then graduated up to a regular gig at The Iron Horse in Westlake Village. The Iron Horse was a pseudo-British pub--a pretty shoddy approximation of a British pub, all things considered, but its Californian patrons didn't know that. As far as they were concerned, it was the perfect fit for Anne and I. There was a small stage in the corner, not far from the bar. It was consistently packed and had a fantastic atmosphere. Once again, it was the tips that sustained us. We discovered that the fact that we were British was a selling point, something that our American audiences found endearing, and so naturally we milked it for all it was worth. Our accents were a charm offensive unto themselves--in particular, I found that the way I spoke helped to sell the punchline of that embarrassing Arby's story, which I wound up telling hundreds of times. The Iron Horse was a great little venue. The shows we put on there were relatively low stakes, but the energy of the place was lively and infectious. That was the job where we learned the most about the differences between American and European audiences.

Our first objective, in getting accustomed to our new surroundings, was to master the ins and outs of tipping culture. We were able to achieve this goal with the aid of a few unlikely allies. One was Billy Joel, whose song "Piano Man" became a staple of our sets at The Iron Horse, mainly due to that line about putting "bread in my jar," which had a way of getting audience members to get up from their barstools and open their wallets. The other was my younger brother, Peter. He was no older than 10 or 11, still in school. I happened to know that he was taking a metalwork class, so we asked him to make us a miniature basketball net. He whipped one up in no time, and we installed it atop an ice bucket. That became our tip jar. Let me tell you, every time we belted out that "bread in my jar" line, the wadded-up bills came raining down. It was incredible. There's nothing an intoxicated person loves more than successfully pulling off a minor feat of hand-eye coordination. Thanks to a mix of generosity and drunken showing off, that ice bucket filled up to the brim more often than not. We went from making $50 a night to making $250 in tips. Anne came up with all sorts of funny, effective ways of egging the audience on. If somebody's shot missed, she'd tell them, "That's no good, you're doing it all wrong, the one dollar bills are too light--try crumpling up a five dollar bill, they're *much* heavier."

One night at The Iron Horse--a slow night, when our tip jar was close to empty and the bar was uncommonly quiet--Anne and I got one hell of a surprise. There were just a few people scattered across the bar, watching us play, and only one of them was doing so with any real attentiveness. He was sitting near the back, clearly alert but keeping himself to himself. Still, it was gratifying to know that we weren't just playing to the wall. Long after Anne and I had given up on anything coming along to alleviate our boredom, and just as we were preparing to call it a night, this stranger approached the stage. The moment he emerged into the pool of light that fell over the stage, we recognized him as David Soul from *Starsky and Hutch*. He asked us if we played any original music, and we were pleased to be able to reply in the affirmative, once we shook off our starstruck silence. We played a couple of our tunes for him, and then he left the bar. To our delight, he then immediately returned, sporting a guitar he'd retrieved from his car. Anne and I stuck around later than we'd planned, that slow, quiet night at The Iron Horse, playing our music with TV's Hutch. It was at once wonderful and surreal––that was LA in the 1980s for you.

CHAPTER 18:
COMMUNICATE

*The English accent is so noble that you can say some of the most undignified things and still sound grand —***Hugh Laurie**

* * *

As memorable as that night was, it's perhaps for the best that the original songs that Anne and I cooked up together were good for more than just jamming with David Soul--if that was as far as our music had taken us, we'd likely still be playing at The Iron Horse to this day. Our tunes also caught the attention of Bob and Michelle Weitz, a lovely married couple who occasionally frequented the bar. It was our original work, rather than our covers, that cemented our business relationship with them--and, more importantly, served as the catalyst for the thirty-five-year friendship we've shared.

Bob, back when we met him, was a frustrated musician himself--frustrated because he was still recovering from an injury that had rendered him incapable of playing the guitar. He had been operating a circular saw and had accidentally sawed into the palm of his left hand, severing a number of nerves and tendons and severely impairing his manual dexterity. At the time, it seemed like a foregone conclusion that his guitar-playing days were over. He and his wife were established and successful musicians who had played in a band called White Rose. Michelle was a brilliant vocalist. Bob's musical abilities, thankfully, extended beyond the guitar, and so he was able to maintain a foothold in the industry even after his accident. He was an amazing sound engineer, and he possessed both an ear for talent and a good head for business. All three of these skills would serve Anne and I well as we got to know and work with the two of them.

Bob had turned his attention to producing records, and it was with him that Anne and I cut our first album, which we dubbed *Communicate*.

If you'd asked me then what I thought of it, I would have told you that it was a first-rate record and that we were really onto something––in hindsight, I'm not so sure. I don't think it matters that my enthusiasm for what we were trying to accomplish with *Communicate* has waned over the years, though. I can still access my impression of how it felt to record the thing and the passion and enthusiasm that we all poured into it. The passage of time and my own shifting standards can't do anything to tarnish those memories, which I will always treasure. I remember being in Bob's studio and seeing my Mum, Jamie-Lee and Wesley in the control room watching Anne and I record the vocals for the album. Nine of the ten songs on the album were written by the two of us. One thing *Communicate* did do, without a doubt, is preserve a precious, fleeting moment in time. I still throw it on every now and again when I'm reminiscing, and it never fails to take me back. I can still recite the track listing by heart:

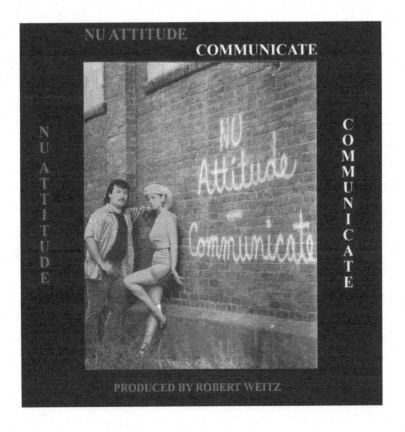

Communicate

1. We're Not Ordinary Lovers

2. Who Am I Now?

3. Lonely Man

4. Please Don't Go

5. Baby

6. Communicate

7. Just You Wait and See (The Troubadour Song)

8. Christmas (Maybe Someday)

9. Over the Rainbow

10. Was It Love?

The Christmas Song on that album became *our* family Christmas song. At some point in our lives, all my brothers and sisters have sung that song together and reminisced about Christmases long gone. I doubt that some of them still hold fond memories any more, but I'm pretty sure a few of us still do. I know that I do.

I might not be able to make it through all ten of those tracks without wincing once or twice when I hear something that wouldn't cut the mustard with me nowadays. But you're only young once, after all, and the fond smiles always win out over the winces. It's important to have a little humility when it comes to these things--every artist, I'm sure, wishes they could take one more pass at their early work, just to scrub away this or that imperfection. But I'm glad that Anne and Bob and I couldn't hear the flaws back then that are so apparent to me now. It made finishing the album so much easier for us to celebrate. I wouldn't dream of robbing our younger selves of that celebratory moment, even if I could. That record is a time capsule in countless ways. Initially we settled on the name Altitude for our band, but that was short-lived. We eventually became known as Nu Attitude––a very eighties name for us to adopt, right down to the spelling!

In addition to producing *Communicate*, Bob and Michelle took an active role in guiding our career more generally. One day, they came to us with enticing news about an upcoming audition in Ontario, California, for V.E. Music, a renowned agency that booked the entertainment for the prestigious and profitable Red Lion hotel chain. We didn't have the slightest clue what to expect, and we knew that we were taking a wild shot in the dark, but we went to the audition regardless. Putting your art into the world means going out on a limb and getting in over your head. You have to be willing to risk looking ridiculous if you ever want to get anywhere. We owed it to ourselves to take a swing at it––and we owed it to Bob and Michelle, who'd been good enough to bring it to our attention.

We showed up to the audition with our cheap, flimsy gear and our battered old equipment, and saw at once that we were out of our depth. The venue, a massive convention room, was swarming with big-name bands sporting high-end gear that put our modest equipment to shame. All the bands set up their equipment around the perimeter of the banquet room. We felt dwarfed by them in a very literal sense. It would have struck us as comical if we hadn't been so nervous. Anne lost her nerve and told me she wanted to sneak off before our number was called. "We can't go on, Terry. Let's just pack up and get out of here."

I understood where she was coming from. It's tempting to want to keep your dignity intact. There are few things more humiliating than a bad audition. But dealing with regret, and asking yourself what might have been, for years after the fact, is even worse. So we decided to stay and reminded ourselves that we had something going for us that our competitors did not. "Let's go on," I told her, "let's talk. The accent–– they'll love the accent. Just play, just do what you do. They'll love it."

And so we did. The person running the audition was a guy named Eric Johannson. To our amazement, he was impressed by our performance and said that he was ready to book us on the spot. I'm certain this unexpected coup was down to a mix of our British accents (which we played up heavily) and the killer Beatles medley we performed. His one concern, he told us, was our outdated equipment. He asked us if we had a decent, modern drum machine. Anne and I knew that this could be our big break, provided we didn't screw it up and let it slip through our fingers.

So I lied, without a second's hesitation or a trace of regret. "Oh, we've got better gear back home," I said. "Our drum machine is broken, so we didn't bring it. But don't you worry, it's a quick fix." I suppose you do what you have to do when opportunity knocks. Anne somehow managed to keep a straight face. Eric nodded, considered a moment, and gave us the gig.

And with that, we had secured our first six-week contract at the Hanford House Red Lion in Richland, WA. I loaned some money off my Mum the following day so that Anne and I could buy a decent drum machine to take on the road with us. We also sprang for a new Yamaha DX7 keyboard to complement our older Fender Rhodes and Roland Juno 106. Six weeks of reliable income at a Red Lion hotel was a godsend for us, and we were deeply grateful. Had we known then that those six weeks would somehow transform into six years as if by magic, I think our souls would have left our bodies.

Bob and Michelle are still in our lives. Bob astonished everyone by working back into guitar-playing shape. He and his wife are now in a Fleetwood Mac tribute band called Mirage, and we represent them at TAD Management.

Now that we are booking shows for them, we have come full circle from the days when they produced that first album of ours. I'm glad that I got the chance to see firsthand what a great guitarist Bob is. His sound engineering skills aren't going to waste either--he still works in Hollywood quite a lot. Which I find rather fitting. Because all of this--that first meeting at The Iron Horse, auditioning for Eric, Bob's miraculous recovery--feels to me as improbable and as inspiring as something straight out of a Hollywood movie.

CHAPTER 19:
LION TAMERS

We make a living by what we get, but we make a life by what we give
—Winston Churchill

* * *

I can still remember the rush I got, the exhilaration of embarking on a new adventure, as we hit the road for eastern Washington. Prior to the Red Lion gig landing in our laps, our experience of the US had been limited to southern California. As we drove out of Los Angeles, the traffic thinned out, and the tangled network of busy streets gave way to straight, open interstates. Anne and I were both in the grips of an excitement that was so palpable that it didn't even bear commenting on. The blue sky yawned colossally overhead as we put LA's skyscrapers in our rearview mirror. I felt at once incredibly small and vested with great significance. Compared to the immensity of the sky and the landscape, I was nothing--but my future lay ahead of me, and it was every bit as immense as the wide open country through which we were driving, and it was bursting with possibility and promise.

We had packed our bags with all the usual road trip essentials, including a big paper map. On this map, Los Angeles and the Tri-Cities were only about six inches apart. *Six inches,* I thought. *That ought to be about half a day's drive... maybe less, if we don't make too many stops.* I needn't tell you how ignorant I felt when that trip I'd been reckoning in hours wound up taking multiple days--at least two, as I recall. It's true that I was no longer dazzled by Arby's signs, but I still had much to learn about America--about the extraordinary scope of the place, the way that you can lose days of your life trekking through fields and valleys that seem to go on forever. Anne and I had little to do on that first trip out of California but take in the natural splendor and savor our shared sense of anticipation. It was such a big country--so much bigger than either of us had imagined. Miles and miles passed beneath our wheels. We tore up the west coast of the US like there was somebody chasing us. Winding roads, unbending freeways, majestic scenery--we saw it all. Every turn brought something new and unexpected, from quaint roadside diners to the breathtaking vistas of the Rocky Mountains, and everything under the sun was awash in a sense of newness. We sang aloud to classic road trip tunes, swapped stories and jokes, and marveled at the beauty of the world around us. Our minds and hearts were open to all of it.

Our Red Lion days had begun, and we couldn't have been more excited. It was our first big break, and we were determined to make the most of it. The Red Lion Hanford House in Richland, WA was the first hotel that Eric sent us to, and our engagement there proved to be a huge success. The timing was such that when we began our Red Lion career, we were still called Altitude and only changed it officially after the Hanford House gig.

The crowd in Richland loved our music and our whole presentation. If there's anything more stress-inducing than a bad audition, it's a bad concert, and so tension was high the first time we stepped out onstage. But after our Hanford House debut, we knew that we had nothing to worry about. We were thrilled to see people up on their feet, moving their bodies, and having a good time – even the staff got into it. When you've got a spotlight shining in your eyes, you can't tell who's got rhythm and who doesn't, who knows the words and who doesn't, or anything like that. All you're able to get is a general sense of movement, energy, and enjoyment––and it's wonderful. Never more so than when you're in front of a crowd full of strange faces in a place you've never been.

Once again, our accents were an asset. We had a novelty factor, even offstage, and we were keenly aware that this made up a large part of our appeal. I doubt we would have ever landed the Hanford House job in the first place if we hadn't learned how to lean into it. Given our roots in the UK music scene, our sound was unlike anything else in the area. Audiences seemed to really like hearing us talk and sing, and we got a kick out of entertaining them. It made generating banter in between songs a breeze. There was never any dead air at one of our shows, I can tell you that much. And if the novel accents weren't enough to win over the audience, the fact that we were a romantic couple with off-the-charts chemistry probably didn't hurt. I think that being from the UK and the accent was a welcome attraction for the staff at the Hanford House. I know that the two of us were eager to learn more about Americans and their way of life and so we befriended the staff quickly. One particular night, after the gig, we were chatting about foods we missed from the UK, and I brought up chip butties. "What the hell is a chip butty?" was the comment from Linda Parker, the bartender – and still a friend of ours today. I said, "There's no way to describe a chip butty. You just *have* to taste one." Anne and I jumped in the car, went to Walmart, and bought a cheap fryer and a bag of potatoes.

Now, chip butties are unequivocally the epitome of culinary bliss, celebrated for their simple yet profound satisfaction. Picture this: golden, crispy potatoes, freshly fried to perfection, nestled lovingly between slices of buttered, pillowy-soft bread. Each bite offers a symphony of textures—crunchy chips yielding to the tender embrace of buttered bread. What sets chip butties apart is their comforting simplicity. No frills or fuss, just pure, unadulterated delight. The warmth of the chips contrasts beautifully with the cool butter, melding flavors in a way that feels like a culinary hug. Seasoned generously with salt and a splash of malt vinegar, each bite transports you to a realm where every savory morsel is a revelation…..actually, they are just thick french fries (as we call them in the USA) on bread and butter…but they are SO good! And the staff at the Hanford House were hooked on them. I have it on good authority that some of our friends from Richland are *still* eating chip butties to this day!

Our style was lively and upbeat, and our set lists were chock full of current hits and crowd favorites of the 1980s. We never felt that playing covers were a drag at all and we never went through the motions. We put our hearts and souls into every performance. Covering a popular tune is a tricky business––you don't want your version to sound like a carbon copy, but neither do you want it to be unrecognizable. It's harder than it looks, threading that needle, but it's become a specialty of ours over the years. Even after weeks or months of playing the same tunes, songs we know note for note, backward and forward, Anne and I can still find ways to surprise one another.

It was at Hanford House that we met Jack Guier, another living legend of a man, at least where our lives are concerned. He was the kind of person who could light up a room with his energy and enthusiasm. I could see straight off that he was a very authentic guy, though he had a flair for showmanship. He liked hanging around with entertainers, despite not being one himself. I think Anne and I were his kind of people. He had a good twenty or so years on the two of us––he must have been in his mid-40s, or thereabouts, when we met him. Nevertheless, we were kindred spirits. Jack was a tall guy, about 6'4" or so, but otherwise unassuming. He used to sit in the Hanford House's lounge and listen to Anne and I play. There were a handful of times, around the middle of the week, when he was the only one there. He'd tap his foot to our set and then offer to buy us a drink when we were finished. The liquor, combined with his natural gregariousness, led to us getting to know him quite quickly. We talked about music, life on the road, and everything in between. In no time at all he became a close and trusted friend.

Jack was a farmer by trade and a prosperous one, at that. He owned a potato packing farm in Pasco, Washington. You wouldn't necessarily expect a man in that line of work to have much to say to the likes of Anne and I, and vice-versa, but the three of us seemed to never run out of things to talk about. All of his questions seemed to come from a place of genuine curiosity, never mere friendliness. He wasn't the type to just make casual conversation. From the moment he got us talking about *Communicate*, the album we'd recorded with Bob Weitz, our fates were sealed.

"I want to buy it," he said.

"Well, that's great…." I replied, "But we don't have any copies."

I could see at a glance that he was not going to be easily rebuffed. Next came the logistical questions, as his businessman side bubbled to the surface. It would have been almost intimidating if he hadn't been in such good humor about it all. You could tell that he was used to making things happen and getting what he was after once he'd set his sights on something. We explained that we were saving up to manufacture a batch of cassettes. The first cassette, I added, was his for the taking. This was an off-the-cuff remark, just something I said to mollify him, but he seized on it. Every time we grabbed a drink with him after a show, from then on, he had the same burning question. "Where's my goddamn album? I want to buy it!"

Truth be told, the holdup was entirely to do with the state of our finances. We'd recorded an album that we were happy with, and we wanted to be able to share it, but we just didn't have the money to have it duplicated. Eventually, I had no choice but to tell Jack as much.

"Once this gig's over," I said, "we'll be able to afford a bulk order of cassettes. The very first cassette has your name on it, I promise you."

He asked how much it cost to have that sort of thing done. A reasonably innocent question, it seemed to me. "The first batch is $1,500," I told him. "Once we pay it, the cassettes will be printed, packaged up, and sent to us, and we'll have them the following week." Jack seemed to accept that explanation, and we left it at that. What I did not know, when we parted ways that night, was that he had only allowed the subject to finally drop because he had already decided to take matters into his own hands.

The very next night, he swung by the bar to knock back a few beers with us after our set, as usual. This had become something of a ritual for us, a custom that we observed like clockwork. What happened next, however, was not customary. Jack produced a thick wad of money and slapped it down onto the bar.

"That's $1500," he said. "I'm buying that first cassette, and that's what I'm paying for it." Anne and I stammered out a string of bewildered protestations, to which he paid no heed.

"'There's no way we can accept that!"…"

"Take it. I want my goddamn album next week."

Jack paid for the entire batch. That's just the kind of guy he was. He didn't know how to take no for an answer, and he gave to those less fortunate than himself like it was the most natural thing in the world. And he wasn't just throwing his money around to get his way, like so many rich people do. He really wanted to support us. Money was not the main adhesive that held our friendship together, but his generosity was nonetheless extraordinary. That's how *Communicate* came to be mass-produced. We would have gotten around to it eventually, even if we'd never met Jack––but I'm so glad we did.

CHAPTER 20:
FIVE THOUSAND MILES

Grief is the price we pay for love
—Queen Elizabeth II

* * *

Those were, simply put, some of the best days of our lives. We made lifelong friends, played our music to the hilt, and enjoyed the hell out of ourselves. Hanford House was just the beginning, but it set the tone for everything that came after. It made us proud to be part of the Red Lion family--it seemed so improbable to us that we had found ourselves there and that we suddenly had so many doors open to us, so many places to lay our heads. Eric, ever the bearer of good news, was the one who gave us a ring when our six weeks at Hanford House were coming to an end, to tell us that Red Lion wanted more. Anne and I were equal parts exhausted and elated. I asked Eric where we'd be heading next. My assumption was that we had landed another short-term commitment comparable to the one we were on the verge of wrapping up. I was still thinking small--in terms of weeks, or perhaps a couple of months. The same kind of thinking that had caused me to underestimate the inches on the map that had shown us the way to Washington. What Eric said next floored me. Red Lion didn't want us for one more engagement--they wanted to fill our calendar for the remainder of the year.

Eric told us that we were going to be playing at Red Lion venues all across the West Coast of the United States. This was beyond our wildest dreams. We were over the moon and then some. If Eric hadn't already been our agent before, he certainly would have earned the position that day. Anne and I had always hoped to have a busy schedule, but we'd never considered that it could all come together for us so quickly. The rest of that year is a jumble in my memory, a mad whirl of stage lights and headlights and dance floors and roads and hotel rooms. We traveled from city to city, state to state – playing to packed houses, more often than not, and giving it everything we had, even on those nights when the crowd was dead or there was scarcely a crowd at all. As fun as the Belplaya was, I think that first year of gigging for Red Lion was the most fun that Anne and I ever had. We met so many remarkable people, from fellow musicians whose talent we admired to fans who knew all our songs like the backs of their hands. I just can't believe how lucky we were. It was an incredible ride. I wouldn't trade a single moment of it for anything.

Because the Red Lion was not a singular destination, like the Belplaya, but rather a chain of hotels, the skills we'd picked up in Spain weren't always transferable to our new job. Wowing Eric and our employers gave us an unprecedented feeling of security, but it also rendered us more rootless than we ever had been before. We were not employed by Hanford House but by the Red Lion Hotel Chain--and that meant that it was never very long before the rubber hit the road. We seldom got the chance to settle down. This took some adjusting to, unused as Anne and I were to all that travel, and the sheer size of the country to which we'd relocated. But we never lost sight of why we were doing it. We loved the music, the people, and the sense of discovery that came with each new gig. The Red Lion became our home away from home. It was weirdly cozy, considering how often we were on the move, and how fleeting and impersonal it ought to have felt. Ours was a strange, far-flung house--our roof spanned hundreds of miles, our foyer was a dozen different hotel lobbies, and our front lawn was America itself.

Those delirious Red Lion days, wonderful as they were, were not without their difficulties. Staying in touch with Anne's family back home was consistently a major headache. We drove all over the US and put thousands of miles on our odometer, but none of that traveling brought us any closer to them. We got closer to or further from California with every new gig--closer to and further from my mother's side of the family--but England, for our purposes, was always the same distance away. I felt a little guilty about this. We'd moved to America, in part, to be nearer to family members from whom I'd become estranged. And now, as a consequence of that choice, Anne was going through an estrangement of her own. I didn't want that for her, and we did what we could to counteract it. But the different time zones and our busy touring schedule made it inconvenient, and the international phone bills were absolute murder. This was long before cell phones, mind you. Anne and I used to spend over $1,000 a month--a significant portion of our income--just to stay connected with loved ones in Liverpool. It was hard to justify that kind of expenditure, but we knew that we had no other options. Anne could only go a couple of weeks without touching base with her parents and siblings before homesickness started to set in. For a travelling musician who has to stay alert and enthused and help their audience have a good time, that homesick feeling can be deadly. And so, despite the exorbitant cost, we did what we had to do. We called home as often as we could. Anne sometimes spent hours on the phone, between shows, catching up on the latest news and gossip from back in Bootle.

I can still hear the metallic rasping sound of our hard-earned quarters sliding into that narrow slit in the payphone, one after another after another. When we learned that Anne's cousin Ged was battling cancer, that awful rasp became the soundtrack of our lives. It even came to eclipse the music that we played, in our minds. Our hands and our mouths were in America, playing the keyboards and singing into microphones, but our souls were across the sea, standing beside Ged's sickbed. The night he died, we called Liverpool from the hotel. It was a horrendous tragedy. He was quite young––far too young. Our bill, when all was said and done, was roughly equal to the pay we'd received from doing our latest gig. The phones took all of it. If Facebook had only been around, back in the 1980s, we could have seen and heard so much more of Ged, in his final days––and there would be so much more for us to remember, now, looking back. We take modern technology for granted, and we're quick to point out all the societal problems it can cause. But to a pair of grief-stricken musicians far from home, crowded into a phone booth, paying a king's ransom, a minute or two of FaceTime would have been nothing less than a miracle, a mercy, and a feat of science fiction. Ged wasn't our only family member who passed on, around that time. One day we'd get a call, and that was how we'd learn that we'd lost a cousin or an uncle. My cousin, Bernard Hallows also died suddenly around the same time as Ged. It was horrible. There's no other way to describe it. Even the music we were playing didn't make it any easier.

Anne and I faced many challenges during our stint with Red Lion. Challenges that, I suspect, would have defeated either of us, had we tackled them independently. I'm sure they would have been too much for me, in any case. But we had each other, and we overcame them together. The Red Lion may have been a kind of second home to us, a scattered home with many hearths. But our families were never far from our minds. It was a time of growth, a time that made us feel like rock stars and pioneers, and I'm proud to say that we found a way to pursue our dreams without forsaking the family ties that made us who we were. I don't think every musician who makes a living on the road can say that.

CHAPTER 21:
DEVASTATION

An angel in the book of life wrote down my baby's birth. Then whispered as she closed the book, 'Too beautiful for Earth —**Unknown**

* * *

As wounded as we were by Ged's passing, our most gutting loss, during this period, was not of someone on the far side of the ocean. It was 1986, and Anne and I were in Coos Bay, Oregon, playing at another Red Lion establishment and excitedly anticipating the arrival of our first child. Like so many other things in our lives, the pregnancy was unplanned, and yet it made perfect sense. It seemed to fit into the general pattern of our life––it was the latest thread in a tapestry of happiness that the two of us were weaving. But our joy was short-lived. Anne lost the baby after eight weeks. It was an ectopic pregnancy. Losing a child is something that no parent should ever have to experience. The weight of our grief was crushing, and the despair we felt was all-encompassing. It was difficult for me to find the strength to carry on––and Anne was hit harder by it than I was. It was her body that had betrayed her. And she had just lost a cousin to cancer. And she was thousands of miles from home. The emotional toll of all this was towering.

I remember feeling so helpless and lost. I wracked my brain for ways that I might comfort her, and I always seemed to come up empty-handed. We had to leave the hospital and head to our next gig while we were still reeling from the doctor's pronouncements, still spiraling on the inside. Before we checked out, Anne was informed that she was no longer able to have children. That diagnosis robbed us of the only light at the end of the tunnel that we otherwise might have had. Getting back behind the wheel and taking off after another Red Lion paycheck felt like the very last thing we should have been doing. But we did it anyway. I now deeply regret that decision. I should have carved out some time for us to grieve properly. Anne, in particular, deserved that. She had every right to an unhurried recovery, and whatever care she needed to heal as fully as she could. I told myself that we'd be better off if we kept ourselves occupied--I thought that we might be able to bury the pain if we just got back to business as usual, and carried on with our frenetic touring schedule. But that's not how it works. I should have known that. Anne is an extraordinary woman, and she hit the stage mere days later with her trademark skill and panache. I doubt that our audiences ever sensed that anything was amiss. But for the first time in our professional lives, our cheerfulness was only skin deep.

Despite the immense pain that we were in, we found a way to move forward, clinging to each other for support all the while. It would take many years, and the intervention of a medical miracle, before we were able to try and have another child. Had we known at the time what modern science would one day help us to accomplish, our misery would have been alleviated, at least somewhat. But in 1986, it felt like we'd come to the end of the road, as far as parenthood was concerned. It was the single most devastating event in our lives.

One of the only things that brought us any pleasure, during this dark time, was our relationship with our two dogs, Alto and Titch, who we'd adopted before ever setting out for that first Red Lion gig at Hanford House. Alto and Titch were physically mismatched--rather large and rather small, respectively, as their names suggest--but they made a perfect pair, in terms of their personalities.

I've left them out of my life story up till now, partly because it's not easy for me to explain, or even understand, how we were ever able to incorporate them into our jam-packed schedule of Red Lion jobs, but more so because I came to appreciate them in a much deeper way after we lost the baby. They helped fill the void when nothing else did--they were the closest thing we had to children.

That first road trip out of California, the one that I fancied would only take 6 to 8 hours--an hour per inch, give or take, which would have been a safe rule of thumb, had I been holding a map of the UK--our two dogs tagged along. We made the journey in a motor home, the kind with a bed over the cab, and engine parts jutting into the interior, shielded by a sheet of metal. The bed didn't see much use, and that protector did little to insulate us from the heat the engine gave off. It was blazing hot in that RV, the whole way up to Washington. It was the middle of May if memory serves. Anne and I beat the heat by keeping each other distracted, which mainly consisted of cranking up the radio and picking out songs to add to our sets--songs that we liked singing together. Alto, meanwhile, beat the heat by a far more expedient method.

The entire time we were on the road, he sat with his front paws dipping in his water bowl. I don't blame the poor creature--it must have been 100 degrees in that damn RV. As long as I live, I'll never forget the sight of Alto soaking his paws like that. Pets have a way of forcing you to see the humor in situations that might otherwise seem totally dire. Anne and I poured our love into those animals after her pregnancy was found to be ectopic. They could not have possibly known how much they helped us.

Losing the baby also taught me the true value of all those pricey phone calls we'd been budgeting for. For a while, they'd just made me feel rather like I had a hole in my wallet, one that I couldn't patch without feeling heartless. But now I'm grateful for every dollar we spent to maintain those familial bonds. It would have been a terrible mistake to deprive ourselves of those meaningful connections. Your loved ones don't live forever. Sooner or later, a day comes when they're no longer there to pick up the phone.

Everything that we were feeling, both good and bad--our passion for music, our grief for our child, our love for our faraway family members as well as our loyal dogs--got folded into the nonstop frenzy of our life on the road. It depleted us more than I could ever describe. When you dive into the deep end, the way Anne and I did, and commit yourself completely to your artistic craft, there are always things that get lost in the shuffle, things that go neglected. As I see it, this can't be helped. Someone you care about will inevitably wind up seeing less of you than you'd like. There aren't enough hours in the day, and there isn't enough of you to go around. It would have been convenient, and less costly, under the circumstances, for Anne and I to cut ourselves loose from all the people we knew, and tell ourselves that it was just us against the world. But we weren't alone. We had people in our lives who loved us, people who wanted to know where we were, and what we were up to. People who would listen if we wanted to regale them with a funny pet story or confide in them about the child we'd lost. We couldn't drop off the face of the earth without hurting them, as well as ourselves. So we stayed in touch, no matter where we happened to find ourselves from one night to the next. We kept shelling out for the long-distance phone calls and kept consoling one another as best we could.

When the first cellphones started coming out, years later, the ones that were shaped like big bricks, and needed their own batteries and carrying cases, Anne and I were among the earliest adopters. To modern eyes, those devices must look ridiculous, but they were a good investment at the time for people who got around as much as we did. We were able to start making investments like that after a few years of steady Red Lion work. Before long, we'd put enough money aside that we could afford to help Anne's parents buy round-trip plane tickets to the US. Flying them out, after years of only having access to their voices, was a beautiful thing. I know it did Anne a world of good. Bringing them over and having them bear witness to our life in America made the whole situation feel more real, somehow. It wasn't all just some wild, surreal, occasionally sad dream that Anne and I were sharing--even if that's how it often felt to us.

My tendency, for decades now, has been to try and see the rosier side of things. It's easy to forget how good we have it today in terms of the tools available to us. The type of relationship that I have with my son nowadays, the intimacy that we enjoy, wouldn't have been remotely possible in the 1980s. We speak to each other every day. I never have to wonder what he's doing or wonder when I'll hear from him next. I don't have to watch the mailbox like a hawk or stay within earshot of a landline phone, the way my parents and Anne's parents did. It's unthinkable to me that I hardly knew what was happening the whole time my Mum and Dad were getting divorced. Later on, when I lived in Spain, I only spoke to them a few times a year. That, too, is impossible for me to believe. But that was life when I was coming up in the world. It was a much bigger place, not so long ago.

CHAPTER 22:
ONWARD AND UPWARD

The best thing to hold onto in life is each other
—Audrey Hepburn

* * *

The first place that Red Lion dispatched us to after Anne got out of the hospital, was Eureka, California. Not an aptly named town, from our point of view. We didn't have any epiphanies there. Just got along to the best of our ability, bearing the burden of our shared sadness, and never allowing our private pain to interfere with our work. The Eureka engagement did net us a few valuable friendships, which helped to take our minds off what we'd just been through. That leg of our Red Lion journey shaped up to be an especially memorable few weeks. We used to go out to the movies just about every day. As if that weren't enough, two or three nights a week we also hit up the local Blockbuster. If you ask me, there's never been a better decade for movies than the 1980s. Every facet of the entertainment industry was abuzz back then. There was more talent out there than the agents, promoters, and marketers knew what to do with. Anne and I only ever laid claim to a tiny slice of that action in the grand scheme of things. But what a privilege it was just to be able to live during that era, engage with its art, and create some of our own.

Our travels took us all over the place after that. Eventually, we landed at Tamarron, a ski resort in Colorado, and we were finally able to let our guard down a little and get settled for the first time in ages. We had performed at the brand-new Red Lion Property in Durango the previous summer, and it was there that the decision-makers at Tamarron saw us and offered us the winter season at the Ski Resort. It was our first gig away from the Red lion properties for a few years.

The climate in that part of Colorado could not have been less like the Costa del Sol, but being able to stay put in one place for that long did remind me of what it had been like to work at the Hotel Belplaya. It was a refreshing change of pace for us, especially in the wake of the tragedy we'd suffered. I felt as though we'd been running at breakneck speed and were finally getting the chance to slow down, catch our breath, and let our aching muscles relax for a while. Colorado, for us, represented a much-needed reprieve--and it was also, luckily for us, a beautiful part of the country in which to cool our heels.

Work kept us busy, as it always had, ever since we'd joined up with Red Lion. But there was also plenty of time for recreation. Alongside our faithful companions, Alto and Titch, we hit the slopes almost every day. (...and although the dogs were very talented....No, they didn't ski!) The highlight of our tenure at Tamarron was when we flew Anne's parents out to visit us. Despite having just recovered from a heart attack, her father, Bill, was determined to have a go at skiing. He refused to be dissuaded, and to his credit, he gave it his all. We had the presence of mind to grab a camera and capture his harrowing, hilarious descent on video, for the sake of posterity. That footage still makes us laugh, all these years later, every bit as hard as we did when he was careening downhill before our very eyes.

Anne and I drove a white Chevy Camaro during our stay in Colorado. It was a quality automobile, but fate decreed that it would not survive until the end of the season. We learned the hard way that the high altitude in Durango can have unexpected--and explosive--consequences. One morning that Anne's parents were in town, we all piled into the car, which was buried under 12 inches of snow, and tried to start it up. Without warning, flames began shooting out from under the dashboard. Everyone hastily leapt out, fell into the snow, and scrambled to safety. Bill remained in his seat for a few harrowing seconds....looked back at Anne and her Mum, rubbing his hands together as if to warm them...and stated, quite dryly, but with a smirk, *"you can say what you like about the car, but at least it has a great heater"*. Bill was quite the comedian. It was such a quintessentially Liverpudlian way to respond to a crisis that I couldn't help but laugh. Our vehicle burned to the ground that day--and it was uninsured, which compounded our misfortune significantly--but at least we got a good joke out of the whole mess. And, for that matter, a bit of unexpected warmth on a chilly morning. From that point on, however, Anne and I never failed to buy car insurance. Lesson learned.

We loved living in Durango so much, despite the havoc that its high altitude could sometimes wreak, that we bought our first home there--a real log cabin, beautifully constructed and full of character, situated on Saddle Trail. The moment we laid eyes on the place, we fell in love with every inch of it, and knew that we had to make it ours. It was a sprawling structure--4000 square feet.

The living room had a massive fireplace, and there was an expansive deck overlooking the mountains, and the kitchen was big and open and suffused with sunlight, and the bedrooms were all comfortable and spacious. The punchline of this story is that a mix of buyer's remorse and the practical realities of our situation prevented us from ever really planting our flag there. We only slept in the house for one night! As much as we loved that cabin, we knew it didn't make much sense for us to try and keep it. We were on the road too much, traveling from gig to gig, and we had no idea when, if ever, we'd have the time or financial resources to properly maintain a property like that. It would have been a crime to let such a lovely house fall into disrepair and lose the charm that had originally drawn us to it. With great reluctance, we decided to sell it off just a couple of years after buying it. I have so many spectacular memories of our time in Durango--my sole regret is that not enough of them were made under that sturdy log roof.

After Colorado, we embarked on a three-year residency at the Red Lion Hotel in Seattle. The longer that Anne and I worked for Red Lion, the longer our engagements tended to get, and the more we were able to relax and get into a consistent day-to-day rhythm. That consistency made everything immeasurably easier--including hosting relatives from out of town. Visits from Anne's folks became a regular fixture of our lives. She and I began to feel that we hadn't properly broken the seal on whatever city we were staying in if Bill and Fran Riley hadn't flown out to see it. My Dad also started dropping in on us, which cheered me immensely. I didn't want him to suspect that, in choosing to live in the US, I had in any way prioritized my relationship with my Mum over my relationship with him. Seattle also allowed us the opportunity to spend some real quality time with my cousin, Ray. I think, of all my cousins, Ray and I had the closest relationship for the longest time. During those 3 years in Seattle, we would often stay at Ray's house in Bothell and stay up, sometimes all night, simply playing board games. Simpler times, for sure. I don't get to spend much time with Ray these days, but I do love him dearly and enjoy the times when we do connect on a call and quickly fall into our chats, mostly about football.

One time, Anne and I went to Las Vegas along with my Dad and her parents. Vegas is a feast for the senses no matter who you are or where you're from, but to the uninitiated, it can feel like sensory overload. All three of our visitors were gob-smacked by the place. It's always heartening to hit upon some way of bestowing that sense of childlike wonder upon your own parents as an adult. That vacation in Vegas did a lot to lift my spirits. Our timing could not have been better. We were there the day The Mirage opened (ironically, as I write these words, it's soon to be knocked down). Vegas, at the time of our visit, was in the process of emerging from its own long depression. It had been a miserable, seedy, and dangerous place all through the 1970s and into the early 1980s. But by the time Anne and I got there, with our starry-eyed parents in tow, it had become a marvelous playground and a showcase for the talents of musical legends like Liberace, Tom Jones, Robert Goulet, and Engelbert Humperdinck, all of whom we got to see perform live. It felt like a place where resurrections and second chances were possible.

Going to Vegas as a family was the perfect capstone to a decade that had reshaped our lives through a combination of profound joy and intense heartache. Despite the challenges and hardships that the 1980s threw at us, it persists for me, in its totality, as a shining beacon of hope and happiness, a repository of music and memories that have been permanently etched into my heart.

CHAPTER 23:
THE OPPORTUNITY OF A LIFETIME

*Twenty years from now you will be more disappointed by the things t
hat you didn't do than by the ones you did do. So throw off the bowlines.
Sail away from the safe harbor. Catch the trade winds in your sails.
Explore. Dream. Discover —* **Mark Twain**

* * *

In January of 1992, Red Lion offered us a gig at La Posada Resort in Arizona. They
didn't have to tell us twice. It was easy for us to keep taking our marching orders from
them, so long as they kept sending us to such lovely corners of the country. It's not
lost on me how fortunate Anne and I were. Our life was a kind of unending vacation,
a string of exotic getaways in which we were able to earn our keep by doing what we
loved most. La Posada was an opulent Spanish-style resort, nestled in the heart of

Paradise Valley, ringed by cacti and palm trees, with a stunning view of the nearby mountains. It exuded warmth and luxury in equal measure and was a beautiful place to call home, every bit the equal of Tamarron in Colorado or the Belplaya in Spain.

We arrived in the sun-kissed state of Arizona and quickly set about discovering what it had to offer. By night we performed in front of enthusiastic locals, holiday-makers and staff members. By day we lounged beside the resort's one-acre pool until our skin thrummed with the sun's warmth. To say that Arizona was good to us would be an understatement. For one thing, Anne was driving her favorite car that she'd ever driven--a black 1978 Corvette with a red interior. It was a hell of a lot sleeker and sexier than the beat-up love bug that had gotten us out of Spain, that's for sure.

My mother, along with my two youngest siblings, came out to visit us while we lived there. In the time since I'd last seen her, she'd both moved to Philadelphia and separated from Eric. The two of them had lived together in Philly for a while--they had only relocated there in the first place on account of his job--but ultimately, they hadn't been able to make it work. Her marriage to Eric lasted about 8 to 10 years, all told. The specifics of their separation were somewhat murky to me then, and they've been made murkier by the passage of time. All I know is that when my Mum, Jamie-Lee, and Wesley showed up at La Posada, it was just the three of them. Eric had somewhere else to be. My sense was that she'd asked him not to come along. I don't know if she'd formally divorced him yet at the time of our Arizona rendezvous, but whether she had or not, it was obvious to Anne and I that they were going through some serious problems. All of this made me feel like a young, blissfully ignorant RAF recruit all over again. I was out of the loop, just as I had been during her first divorce.

I had come a long way in my career and established both a reputation and a reliable income stream for myself. For all intents and purposes, I was an adult, a man with marketable skills and a good head on his shoulders. But all it took was one visit from my mother to remind me of the confusion and powerlessness of childhood. Life is much more than just the sum total of your decisions. Many things--the biggest things, arguably--are outside of your control. I didn't have a say in whether my parents remained together or who they wound up remarrying. Anne and I hadn't been given a vote when she'd been rendered infertile by a cruel twist of fate. It seemed to me that destiny, or some other nefarious force I didn't understand, was at work in the world and that it had a way of breaking families up, or else, in the case of Anne and I, seeing to it that they never fully formed, to begin with. I always felt that Anne and I would never split from one another--no force on earth could compel us to do that. But I also knew that our family would always be a bit smaller than we wanted it to be. We would always be one member short.

That's when Anne and I received a call that would upend everything for us and change the parameters of what we believed to be humanly possible. Anne's Mum gave us a ring, out of nowhere, to tell us that she'd applied, on our behalf, to the UK's National Health IVF treatment program--and we'd just been accepted. That phone call shattered whatever sense of contentment we'd managed to build up around ourselves in one fell swoop, like a rock thrown through a window. All at once, with the prospect of parenthood once again on the horizon, we felt as though we'd been settling for less than we should have been and that our happiness had been the product of a compromise. Getting that news from Anne's mother both captured our imaginations and put us in a hell of a difficult bind. We'd been gigging for Red Lion for years at that point. The road that lay ahead of us had been wide and sunny--and, increasingly, paved in gold. Suddenly, and without warning, it had forked. We could either remain in America and continue to enjoy the fruits of our labors or return to the UK, where we might have a shot at becoming parents. Having kids wasn't really on our minds that fateful day when the phone rang. We'd already lost one, and that wound was still fresh, still aching. We were living the good life with our two dogs. It was an unencumbered life, a life of freedom, exploration, and nonstop movement. We had everything we could have ever asked for--save for one thing. And that one thing could only be ours if we tossed all the rest of it aside and went back across the ocean. Even then, it would not be a sure thing. If we went back to the UK, we would have to forfeit our comfort and our sense of direction and hang all our hopes on a medical procedure we only dimly understood. The smart play would have been to stay right where we were. But it's impossible to be perfectly rational when you arrive at a certain crossroads in life. Anne and I tried to be sensible and weigh all the pros and cons. But this was a decision, we soon realized, that could only be made with the heart rather than the head. In our hearts, we wanted a child. And in the face of that truth, all the other factors were rendered naught.

The worst part of going back--worse than parting ways with Red Lion – was leaving behind Alto, our beloved Samoyed. He was just too big to make the trip. There was no way we could find to make it safe and feasible. Little Titchy got to tag along with us, but Alto had to be re-homed. We searched for a new family for him, our hearts heavy all the while, and finally found a lovely bunch of people who owned a big farm.

We knew it would make him happy to have so much space to run around and play in all day long. It was the right choice for him, but that didn't make it any easier on us. I wish there were some way to explain your plans to your animal companions--every new development in their lives can only ever come as a complete surprise to them. Titch, speaking of which, might have felt that, of the two of them, Alto was the one that lucked out. Because Titch's fate, in the short term, was the furthest possible thing from frolicking in a wide-open farmyard. Upon our return to England, he had to go into quarantine for six months. I hate to think of how frightening and confusing that must have been for him, but I can take solace in the knowledge that Anne and I visited him just about every week that he was locked away. We used to go to the facility where he was being quarantined and crawl into his kennel on our hands and knees so that we could sit down beside him.

For this, as well as a host of other reasons, the move back to England was deeply bittersweet. We were excited to potentially be starting a new chapter in our lives, but leaving behind our career in the US was hard. We had fostered so many wonderful friendships and made so many unforgettable memories during our time in California, Colorado, Arizona, and elsewhere. It stung us both to find ourselves back in a place where the maps were smaller, where inches translated neatly into hours rather than ballooning into full-blown days. But the prospect of starting a family through IVF was more than we could bring ourselves to pass up. If we had passed on it, we would have regretted doing so as long as we lived. We understood there was a chance that it would all be for nothing, a chance that we might give up everything and gain nothing in return. But it was a chance we both knew we had to take. We packed our bags, said goodbye to the desert paradise we had come to love so much, and took off for England with a renewed sense of hope and purpose. We were going to try IVF--we were going to do everything we could to turn our seemingly unattainable fantasy of parenthood into a reality. A difficult trial awaited us, upon our return to our homeland--but so did the supreme joy of our lives.

CHAPTER 24:
FAZAKERLEY AND SKELMERSDALE

A baby fills a place in your heart that you never knew was empty
*— **Unknown***

* * *

The IVF clinic at Fazakerley Hospital in the early 1990s was a cutting-edge facility that provided hope to many couples struggling with infertility. Anne and I were far from the only people to benefit from the kindness, patience and expertise of the miracle workers who operated there. The clinic offered a range of fertility treatments, including in vitro fertilization, and it was staffed by a team of skilled professionals who were dedicated to helping troubled couples achieve their dream of having a child. The process was not an easy one. Even with professional aid, false starts and dead ends were commonplace. Infertility can be an incredibly brutal and uncompromising condition. You have to be prepared to soldier through one disappointment after another, placing your trust in the doctors to support you and answer your questions with compassion every step of the way--something that they never failed to do, in our experience. For us, as for many other couples, Fazakerley's IVF facility was a ray of light that illuminated a viable path forward--one that was narrow, and long, and arduous, but which might lead, finally, to parenthood.

Every detail of our first appointment is seared into my memory. Anne and I had been waiting for months to be summoned to the hospital. When the call finally came, in February 1993, a confounding mix of incompatible emotions came flooding into us. We were simultaneously reticent, cautiously optimistic, and scared out of our minds. We had so many uncertainties and concerns, and we didn't have the first clue of what to expect. When we finally met with our embryologist, Dr. Martin Smedley, he was exceptionally gentle and patient with us. He took us through the entire process step by step, laying everything out in painstaking detail. We had trouble, as laypeople, understanding everything he had to say, but he broke it all down for us as best he could. His bedside manner was simply incredible. I appreciated that he treated us kindly without coddling us--he was honest about the potential for setbacks and stressed the importance of keeping our expectations low due to the slim likelihood of success. This did little to quash our nervousness, but it did leave us feeling more comfortable and well-informed. We walked out of that appointment feeling like we might one day become parents after all--a possibility that would have been utterly unthinkable to us just one year prior in Arizona.

I cannot say enough good things about Dr. Smedley and his staff. They were so incredibly supportive and compassionate. We felt, at all times, even when the prognosis was grim, that we were in the best possible hands. IVF is a complex and taxing process, one that requires that medical professionals work closely and candidly with their patients in order to achieve the best possible results The first step is ovarian stimulation, which involves a woman's ovaries being stimulated with fertility drugs, causing them to produce multiple eggs. After that, the eggs are retrieved from the ovaries using a small needle, typically under sedation. The retrieved eggs are then mixed with sperm in a laboratory dish, and the fertilized eggs are then allowed to grow into embryos. After a few days, a small catheter transfers one or more embryos into the uterus. The patient then waits for a couple of weeks to find out if the transfer was successful and if pregnancy has occurred. The fact that I can still remember all this is a testament to Dr. Smedley. It was clearly a priority for him that his patients not be kept in the dark. Anne and I always knew exactly what was occurring at every stage of her treatment. Still, at all of the most crucial junctures, she had to bear the brunt of the stress alone. There was only so much I could do to help her shoulder it.

The day of the egg retrieval was about as emotionally turbulent as the ectopic pregnancy had been back in the mid-1980s. There were times when the suspense became so unbearable that my faith began to falter, and I caught myself questioning why we were subjecting ourselves to such a dreadful strain. If the IVF refused to take, and we exhausted all our options, it would be an agony even greater than the loss of the first child had been. I didn't want to imagine how it would destroy us both if we were to get our hopes up, go through all of it, and still emerge childless. This was a fear response on my part. I just wanted us to not be in pain anymore. I needed closure––I needed to know, once and for all, whether parenthood was on the table for us or whether we were just fooling ourselves. How Anne got through it all with her sanity intact, I will never understand. It was nearly more than I could bear––and she had to bear so much more of it than I did. I was sick with worry, watching her undergo the egg retrieval procedure that day. But we both knew that we had no choice but to trust the process and try to have faith in Dr. Smedley and his team. If anyone could make it happen for us, it was them.

When we received the news that we had three embryos ready to be transferred, it gave us a glimmer of hope. The thought that we could have not just one chance at having a child but as many as three was overwhelming. Dr. Smedley opted to trans-fer two embryos, hoping that at least one would take hold. The ensuing wait for the pregnancy test lasted an eternity. Seconds crept by. Days felt like months. There was never a moment when the test was off our minds. It was unrelenting. By the time the results finally came back, Anne and I had both been reduced to twin bundles of raw nerves. Whatever we were going to be made to feel, by the results of the test, we were going to feel profoundly and intensely. Good news would send our spirits heavenward––bad news would lacerate us on the deepest possible level. I took Anne's hand and gave it a reassuring squeeze, and we braced ourselves for Martin's findings.

When he told us that Anne was pregnant, we wept. That moment remains *the* most important moment of our lives. But even as the joyful tears coursed down our faces, we knew the journey was far from over. The closer we got to the end of the gestation period, the more gutted we would be if things somehow went wrong. For nine months, we held tight to hope and to one another. It felt like clinging to a frayed rope suspended above an abyss of disaster.

To make matters worse, things were tough for us financially at this time. In England, there were no cushy resorts clamoring for our music and promising to keep us busy for years at a stretch. After moving to a council house in Skelmersdale, we felt as though we'd been backed into a corner. Suddenly, our future was uncertain. Anne's younger brother, Ste, and his wife, Mel, moved in with us for a while as they, too, were struggling to make ends meet. Ste was always the closest sibling to Anne. He became our roadie while we performed in social clubs, trying to scrape together a living. I'd spent my whole adult life hopping from place to place, starting over more or less from scratch every time I arrived in a new country. It was a gamble that I had always managed to pull off, a coin toss that I seemed to be fated to always win. The gauntlet of IVF treatments was torturous enough without having to worry about keeping the lights on at home. Even if Anne carried our son to term––and we both prayed that she would––what sort of life did he have to look forward to? How would we provide for him?

Bitterness never took root in my heart, however. If this was the price that had to be paid for us to have a baby, then so be it. Better to be hardscrabble parents in England than successful and childless in America. I know that Anne felt exactly the same way. That was the inescapable upside of our return to the UK––the single weight on the scale that balanced out all the bad things.

CHAPTER 25:
MELTING IN THE DARK

How lucky I am to have something that makes saying goodbye so hard
—A.A. Milne

* * *

Our UK homecoming had another silver lining that bears mentioning: I was reunited with my Uncle Harry, that wonderful man who'd always encouraged me to stick with my piano playing when I was a boy. I'd kept in touch with him all through my travels, but seeing him in person always had a different impact. For me, it was a reunion that couldn't have happened at a better time. Winding up in Skelmersdale, after seeing all the extraordinary sights we'd seen, made all our past successes seem terribly fragile to me. We had always just been a few unforeseen setbacks or unwise decisions away from poverty. It was going to be beans on toast for me again, if I didn't choose my next course of action carefully. But as precarious as our situation was, and as close to catastrophe as we seemed to be, I knew there was one yardstick against which I could still measure myself with pride. I could play "MacArthur Park"--and hadn't Harry always told me that he'd know I was a good musician, so long as I mastered his favorite tune?

When we got back to the UK, Harry was one of the first people I went to visit. He and his wife Barbara lived in Morecambe. He'd left the lorry-driving business behind by then, and bought his own fish and chip shop—Harry's Chippy, he called it. It's still regarded as the finest fish and chip shop in the history of Morecambe. The food they served there was just plain amazing—and my auntie worked her arse off, seven days a week, to make sure it stayed that way. Her work ethic and Harry's larger-than-life personality were an unbeatable combination. They had lines out the door every single night without fail.

Harry truly was a one-of-a-kind individual. His health suffered more and more as time went on, but he remained the big character he'd always been, right up to the very end. In the years that followed our return to the UK in the early 1990s, we saw a lot of him and Barbara. We've been on multiple cruises together, and he visited us in Mexico, when we had a house down there. It was always a joy to kick back and luxuriate with him, after Anne and I rebounded and established lasting success for ourselves, because he'd seen us at a point in our lives when that kind of future seemed to be slipping beyond our reach. It really is impossible for me to convey just how important he is to me. Out of everyone in my parents' generation, with the exception of my mum and dad, he's the most influential figure for me, and the person to whom I became the closest. I never knew him to be anything other than an unwavering pillar of love, support and guidance. Without his presence in my life, I would be a wholly different person.

When Harry and Barbara celebrated their fortieth wedding anniversary, Anne and I went back to Morecambe to help them celebrate. We sprang a surprise performance of "MacArthur Park" on them at the anniversary party. Harry, Barbara, Anne and I were all moved deeply—the song held great meaning for him, of course, but I wonder if he could have possibly known how much it meant to me. Playing it for him that day in Morecambe and seeing his tears flow made me feel at once like a little boy, eager to impress his favorite uncle. Few experiences in my life have been more creatively and emotionally satisfying for me than performing that song for Harry and showing him what his years of encouragement had done for his nephew. He transformed my life in ways that I could never hope to adequately repay him for, and I know without a doubt that I'll never be able to listen to that song without thinking of him.

Harry passed away on December 30th, 2023. I made the decision to go and see him just two or three weeks before he passed. Anne and I discussed it, beforehand. It was the easiest decision imaginable, and I will forever be glad that I made it. We knew that he had a limited amount of time left. I feel strongly that it's better to pay your respects while a person is still living rather than waiting until they've passed on. Kind words are wasted on caskets. Instead of waiting until after his death, I got to spend time with him while he was not only still alive but still alert––still himself. We were together for four or five days, and he was perfectly cogent the entire time.

Our topics of conversation ranged from love to truck driving to karaoke and anything else he felt like touching on. I let him take the lead––and I was happy to follow anywhere that he led me because his life had been so full and because I knew I wouldn't get another chance to hear him talk about it. It made my heart swell, knowing that I wasn't just going back there to look at a body. What could have been a regretful graveyard monologue instead became a conversation.

I didn't go to his funeral, ultimately. Anne and I were in Antarctica at the time. I wish I'd been able to attend, but being prevented from doing so was made so much easier by my decision to spend that precious time with him a few weeks prior. In a sense, I had already said goodbye.

Just before I turned to leave, the last time I saw him, he beckoned me over to him. The expression on his face told me that he had something to impart, something he had been dwelling on for a long time. His very last words to me after I returned to his side were simply this: "Don't forget Barbara and Karen."

As far as I'm concerned, that tells you everything you could ever wish to know about the kind of man he was. His parting words to me were an act of kindness for someone other than himself. He wanted to be sure, before he died, that his wife and daughter would be looked after and that Anne and I would stay involved in their lives. I think he must have known that we would have done that regardless, but it's still a testament to his generosity of spirit that his mind was on them rather than himself. He didn't care what became of him––his priority was seeing to it that I would do what I could to help fill the hole that his imminent passing would create in the lives of his loved ones.

That was the kind of man I wanted to be––the kind of man I wanted my son to be once he came into the picture. The IVF treatment that Anne went through after we moved back to the UK yielded nothing short of a miracle for her and I. But reentering my uncle's orbit served as a kind of companion miracle for me. It was a useful reminder of all the goodness I wanted to model for my offspring––all the goodness Harry had given me. I miss him so much.

CHAPTER 26:
GIGS AND GAMES

Where we love is home - home that our feet may leave, but not our hearts
—Oliver Wendell Holmes, Sr.

* * *

Once Anne and I felt reasonably sure that the pregnancy was real and lasting and could be relied upon--that it wasn't just going to cruelly vanish on us, the way the last one had--we traded one form of fear for another. We went from worrying that Nick would never be born, to worrying about the sort of life he had to look forward to, after his birth. For me, the pregnancy created a kind of countdown, an hourglass with nine months' worth of sand in it. We were newly arrived in England, and we had the better part of a year to work like mad and shore up some funds for our son's arrival. We had essentially no safety net when we abandoned America and moved back--but what else was new? That was the way we had always done it. Only this time, we had something bigger than ourselves to fret over. That changed everything for us. This time, we knew, would have to be the last time. We needed to put some real money away.

Our gear was old, and we owned an older transit van. All still usable, albeit undesirable. Our main source of work during this uncertain time came from an agent based in Preston named Graham Fletcher. Graham was known to be a bit of a rogue, but he managed to get us a lot of gigs, so his rascally side couldn't have been interfering all that much with his trade--I have a feeling that his trademark roguish charm might have even been a professional asset for him. The gigs that we got from Graham fell into two discrete categories. There were the "pick up" gigs, which paid out the night of the performance, sometimes directly and sometimes through the agent, and then there were the far less appealing "no pick up" gigs, which paid out at a later date. Bookings were always defined in advance by which of these two types of gigs they were, so there was no confusion. That was the idea, anyway. I remember one gig in particular when the boundary was blurrier than any of us would have liked.

This show was in Wigan, not too far from where we lived. We were flat broke and thankful to have scored a gig in our neck of the woods, as we had no money for petrol. Anne, Ste and I had to dig down the back of the couch looking for loose change so that we could scrape together enough fuel money to get us to the venue. It was a "pick-up gig" (or so we were told), and so we expected to be paid either before the show or just afterward. To our horror, however, when we asked for our payment at the end of the night, the concert secretary told us that we had, in fact, just played a "no pick up" gig. Any musician would have been disappointed to learn of this mix-up. We were more than disappointed--we were devastated. We'd driven out to Wigan on fumes and had, as far as we knew, stranded ourselves there. It's a miracle that we were able to make it home that night. We had no choice but to chance it. The needle was sitting on empty all the way.

Despite this setback and several others, we remained resilient and continued to play gigs. That was the world we knew, the world we understood. I would have become a dockworker or bricklayer or anything under the sun, if that's what it had taken, to get things situated before our child came along. But music was where my talent resided. As rough and tumble and unreliable as it could sometimes be, it was still the best way for me to make consistent money. But I couldn't have done it alone. Not with a baby on the way. Without Anne's musical abilities, emotional support, and inner strength, and without Ste lending a helping hand, I wouldn't have stood a chance. We made it happen together.

Still, we needed multiple income streams if we were going to ever start to feel truly secure financially. Anne and I started throwing around different ideas for possible business ventures. Things we might do to earn a passive income, one that didn't require so much running about, so much blood, sweat and tears. Looking back, I can safely say that we only ever cooked up two good business ideas, and that happened when we put our heads together. There were plenty of other ideas that weren't so hot--I'm forced to conclude that all of them came from me, and me alone, without Anne's involvement. The first of the two good ideas that I want to touch on is NAP Music.

When she and I first landed back in the UK in 1992, backing tracks were beginning to take off. We were savvy enough to recognize that there was money to be made by capitalizing on that technology, which was becoming a mainstay of the recording industry. "Why don't we start making backing tracks for other artists?" Anne asked me one day. "We're already doing it for ourselves." I couldn't argue with her logic. We borrowed fifty pounds from Anne's mother shortly after making landfall in England and spent it on a new cassette player--the only new piece of equipment we had at our disposal, which ought to tell you how much faith we had in this fledgling business of ours. In a rather extraordinary twist of fate, the first person who hired me to create a backing track for him was Pat O'Hare, the very same man who'd handpicked me to fly off to Spain and work at the Belplaya. It felt to me like an entire lifetime had elapsed since the last time I'd seen and done business with him. That's how NAP Music started--that was the foundation upon which everything else was built. All that Anne and I were trying to do was diversify our operation and change with the times, but we do have a right to be proud of the forward-thinking approach we adopted. We were the first company to offer tracks in multiple keys, which really helped to elevate us above our competition. Having a good idea is the first step. Executing it well is the second, harder, costlier step. But somehow, we managed it, thanks to Pat O'Hare and Anne's mum.

Once I had a bit more money in my pocket, I was able to let my guard down and start to enjoy England's simple pleasures once again. As a die-hard Manchester United fan since boyhood, getting back to Old Trafford was one of my top priorities upon our return. I couldn't wait to experience the vicarious thrill of watching the Reds play again, win or lose. My first game, after my long sojourn through Spain and the US, was on September 2nd, 1992. United faced off against Crystal Palace that day. The excitement in the air was palpable from the moment I entered the stadium, and once the game got underway, it only ratcheted up further. I felt like I was home again. The adrenaline pumping through my veins was the perfect complement to the electricity in the air all around me. United won 1-0, that crisp September evening--though the game is more widely remembered nowadays not for its score but for Dion Dublin breaking his leg.

Being back in the stands, watching my favorite footballers play, made all the years I'd spent abroad melt away. As the 1992 season progressed, United kept playing brilliantly. They had narrowly missed out on the title the year before, but I had a good feeling about them all the way through 1992 and into 1993--and I wasn't the only one. You could sense the communal goodwill that my fellow Manchester United fanatics and I all shared, the yearning we felt for them to eke out one victory after another and go all the way to the top. And then it happened. On November 26th, United signed Eric Cantona, and everything changed. His arrival brought a brand new dimension to United's attacking options. His skill, flair, and borderline supernatural ability to score spectacular goals made him an instant hit with the fans, myself included. I was thunderstruck by my own luck, having come back to the UK just in time to bear witness firsthand to an exciting new era for my favorite team.

Signing Cantona sparked a legendary run that would see the Reds go unbeaten for the next twelve games. They won ten of those games and drew two. It was nothing less than a rampage, and it was more than enough to propel them into the upper echelons of that season's Premier League table. They scored 67 goals in 42 games, more than any other team that season. Their defense was the equal of their offense–– they conceded just 31 goals, the fewest of any team in the league. Even though I did nothing more than cheer them on, I somehow felt that I was contributing, in some infinitesimal way, to all this success––that some portion of it, however small, belonged to me. That's what it means to be a United fan.

United's title win was sealed on May 2nd, 1993 when they beat Aston Villa 1-0 at Old Trafford. Steve Bruce, the captain of the team, scored the winning goal. He had been one of United's standout players that season, and he brought it to a fitting and rousing conclusion. United hadn't won a league title since 1967, and the 1980s had not been kind to them. But I, along with countless others, never lost faith in them–– and that faith was rewarded a hundredfold when my return to England coincided with that astonishing 1992-1993 season, the season that kicked off their glory years.

CHAPTER 27:
WELCOME, NICK

"Making the decision to have a child is to decide forever to have your heart go walking around outside your body" — Elizabeth Stone

* * *

Anne and I kept performing all through her pregnancy, and it soon became apparent to us that our unborn child had inherited our shared love of music. It was like we were already a kind of musical trio. After our shows, she'd fill me in on the part of the performance I'd missed--the part that had been happening inside her belly. He used to kick and move around whenever he heard music playing. No small wonder, then, that music ultimately became such a huge part of his life. We often joke that he has it in his veins. Anne and I felt comfortable sticking to our busy schedule because the pregnancy, despite how hard it had been to come by, and how precious it still felt, was relatively low stress--at least, up to a point. That started to change around the eighth month, when Anne began suffering from extreme heartburn and vomiting. Ordinarily this would not have been cause for alarm, but after all the anticipation and uncertainty we'd been through, it was more than enough to raise alarm bells for the two of us.

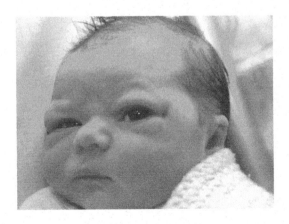

Our son was due to be born on November 11th, 1993. That was the date we were given. Fate, however, had slightly different plans in store for us. Anne didn't go into labor until the 15th. If her body had held out much longer, I think it's likely that they would have induced her. Our excitement and nervousness was stratospheric at this point. All I wanted was for the three of us to cross the finish line together as smoothly and painlessly as possible--Anne, and the baby, and me. I had to trust her body to know when it was ready. Given what a struggle it had been for us to conceive, that trust ought to have been harder to come by. But I had the sense that our suffering would soon be behind us. I think Anne and I were together for every single minute of those extra four days.

A day or two before Anne finally went into labor, we met with Martin Smedley, her embryologist, and had a relaxed conversation in which he explained to us, for the umpteenth time, what to expect. We asked him, in passing, how many IVF births he'd taken part in. He estimated that Nick was roughly his hundredth. Anne and I thought that was incredible. Here was this humble man who had changed hundreds of lives, including our own. Gradually, the conversation shifted away from medical necessity and into more personal terrain. We asked him what seemed to us to be a logical follow-up question, though it might strike you as somewhat random. How many of those hundred kids, we asked, do you still see? It took him a moment to respond. He seemed slightly taken aback. "Well," he said, "none of them, really."

We were speechless. He went on to clarify that he was involved in one of their lives, but only in a professional capacity, because he was sick and frequently hospital-ized. Beyond that, he had no point of contact with any of them. I don't want to sound unduly judgmental because there are valid reasons for any parents to have made a different decision than the one that we eventually made. Perhaps they saw their embryologist as an unemotional expert and nothing more--perhaps they thought it would be inappropriate to try and break down those doctor/patient barriers and get to know him as a person. Regardless, something about it didn't sit right with either of us. We agreed that when the time came, we would find some way to show Martin how much we appreciated his work. The time came just a few nights later.

On November 16th, 1993, at 4:04am, my life was changed permanently and for the better. It might be more accurate to say that it was completely turned upside down. I had been looking forward to being a father for years, and by then--a small part of me had held onto that hope even when it seemed beyond the realm of possibility—but that desire for fatherhood that I had felt, strong and sincere as it was, was just a faint shadow compared to the depth of feeling that came flooding into me, on the day my son was born. Love that powerful changes your personality. It influences the way you perceive everything and forever alters the workings of your imagination. I'm not the same man I was before. Holding my newborn son in my arms was like being reborn myself.

As I held him, I was overcome with an indescribable combination of emotions that clashed and churned inside me like an admixture of volatile chemicals. Joy, fear, pride, and wonder filled my heart as I beheld the tiny, beautiful human being that Anne and I had created with Dr. Smedley's help. When the weight of my responsibility hit me, it was a miracle I didn't crumple to the floor. I think that I only remained standing for my son's sake. He was relying on me to feed and shelter him, to shape and guide him as he grew, to nurture his body and mind, and to usher his development along. Every bit as colossal as my sense of paternal duty was the profoundness of the love I felt for Anne at that moment and the depth of my appreciation for the beauty and fragility of life.

The first name that Anne and I settled on was TJ, but at some point, not long before his birth certificate found its way into our hands, we tossed that name out and went with Nickolas. There was no debate between us as to what his middle name should be--we both agreed that it had to be Martin, in honor of the incredible doctor without whom none of this would have been possible. It was the perfect choice. In that moment, it simply felt right to us. It still does. When Dr. Smedley saw our baby boy's birth certificate, with his full name printed on it, his eyes welled up with tears. Every year on Nick's birthday, for the following six years--the duration of our stay in England--the three of us dropped by Dr. Smedley's office and spent half an hour or so with him. This became a cherished ritual. I believe it meant a great deal to Dr. Smedley--I know that it meant a great deal to us.

I'm not claiming that Martin became a third parent to Nick, or anything like that. We only saw the man once a year. But Nick grew up knowing that a third person, in addition to his mum and dad, had taken an active role in his creation. We didn't expect him to grasp the finer points, of course--some of the science was beyond even us. The important thing was for him to understand that people like Dr. Smedley, people who do good in the world, deserve respect and recognition and to see the fruits of their labors up close.

We lost track of Dr. Smedley for a long time after we left England. To my everlasting delight, we were able to re-establish contact with him shortly before Nick got married. He and Nick and Nick's bride-to-be, Julia, had a Zoom call together on the eve of the wedding. You simply never know when or how the most important people in your life will enter or reenter it. It was the opportunity of a lifetime to watch Dr. Smedley work and to walk with him right up to the cutting edge of what science can do. But for all his professionalism and expertise, Anne and I never lost sight of the human being underneath--and we made sure that our son never lost sight of that human being either.

CHAPTER 28:
MY LITTLE MIRACLE

Any man can be a father, but it takes someone special to be a dad
—Anne Geddes

* * *

I've played a lot of varied roles in my life. This is something that all of us must do. We all have to be different things to different people at different times. I've been a son to my parents, a brother to my siblings, a husband to Anne, and I'm happy to say, a friend to more people than I can count.

Simply put, however, being a father is the most important role I have ever been called upon to play. Nothing else comes close. I've worked hard to become a good Dad and role model, which has sometimes required me to go against the grain, but I would say that I've done a halfway decent job. Perhaps my own assessment isn't worth all that much, though. Answering that question, ultimately, isn't something I can do. That task must fall to Nick. But when I look at the way he turned out and the kind of man that he matured into, I can't help but feel like I must have been doing something right all those years.

Somebody told me once that you cannot be both a father and a friend. What they meant by this, I gather, is that it's a father's duty to reject the latter role, no matter how much it pains him, in order to succeed in the former role. I have to say, I could not disagree more. My son has recently turned thirty, at the time of this writing, and he's my best friend in the world. Every minute of friendship that we've shared has enriched my life. We can talk to one another about our problems as though we were good mates. There are times when our closeness is such that even the generational gap between us starts to feel like it's shrinking. In those moments, it's almost as if we're a pair of boyhood pals, and I've known him and loved him for longer than he's even been alive. What's really remarkable is that this unique friendship of ours has done nothing to detract from our equally extraordinary father-son relationship. If you've ever experienced that sort of bond, you don't need me to tell you how special and invaluable it is. Whatever side of the equation you're on, whether you're a son or a father, my advice is the same: embrace it with both hands and never let it go. No other experience in my life, no other happiness, no other victory, can measure up to the experience of being Nick's Dad.

There's an old poem by Edgar Guest that expresses my parenting philosophy better than I can. These words resonate with me every day:

> Be more than his dad
> Be a chum to the lad;
> Be a part of his life
> Every hour of the day;
> Find time to talk with him
> Take time to walk with him,
> Share in his studies
> And share in his play;
>
> Take him to places
> To ball games and races,
> Teach him the things
> That you want him to know;
> Don't live apart from him
> Don't keep your heart from him,
> Be his best comrade
> He's needing you so!

Never neglect him
Though young, still respect him,
Hear his opinions
With patience and pride;
Show him his error
But be not a terror,
Grim-visaged and fearful,
When he's at your side.

Know what his thoughts are
Know what his sports are,
Know all his playmates,
It's easy to learn to;
Be such a father,
That when troubles gather
You'll be the first one,
For counsel, he'll turn to

You can inspire him
With courage, and fire him
Hot with ambition
For deeds that are good;
He'll not betray you
Nor illy repay you,
If you have taught him
The things that you should.

Father and son
Must in all things be one –
Partners in trouble
And comrades in joy.
More than a dad
Was the best pal you had;
Be such a chum
As you knew, to your boy.

Raising Nick, right from the beginning, was an absolute joy. It brought all sorts of memories of my own boyhood bubbling to the surface. Things I'd half-forgotten, along with things I still recalled vividly. One especially vivid memory of my childhood was my experience of watching the moon landing in 1969. Only one house on our street in Openshaw had a television. A small black-and-white TV that only had two channels—–BBC One and BBC Two, the only two channels in England, back then. Somebody lugged that television outside, onto the street, with a cord running back into their house so that everyone on the block could huddle together and watch Neil Armstrong set foot on the lunar surface. I must have been about eight years old at the time. Nine at most. When I first looked into my infant son's wide, inquisitive eyes, so full of curiosity, I couldn't help but start to wonder about all the historical events that he would live through and all the memories that he would form. What, I wondered, would his moon landing be? We were on the verge of a new millennium, but just as with any period of history, it was impossible to know for certain just what was around the corner. I made a conscious effort to reconnect with my memories of the things in my own youth that had made me feel safest and happiest so that I could recreate those feelings for my son. I wanted to be everything for him that my role models had been for me and more. My goal was to embody my mother's best qualities, my father's best qualities, and my uncle's best qualities all rolled into one.

The morning Nick was born, a melody started running through my head—– one that felt like it had been with me for a long time but which I couldn't quite place. I'm not sure that I was fully aware, in my overjoyed and sleep-deprived state, that I was not remembering a melody I'd heard before, but rather inventing something that sounded familiar to me only because it sprang out of the deepest part of my heart. A couple of days after we brought Nick home from the hospital, I decided to put lyrics to this melody. The name I soon settled on was "My Little Miracle."

This is how it went:

MY LITTLE MIRACLE
I can't believe this precious gift
More dear and pure than gold
With your little toes to play with
And your tiny hands to hold

131

You're my sunlight, my nighttime
My happiness and tears
All wrapped up in a rainbow
With all my hopes and fears

Nickolas, you're my baby boy
You're my pride and joy
You're everything I have lived for
Nickolas, all my dreams are different now
You've got to me somehow
You're my little miracle
You're my little miracle

Each time I hold you in my arms
And hum a song or two
There's nothing more to wish for
All the world belongs to you
Each time I see that boy of mine
Sleeping in his crib
My emotions overcome me
He's the reason that I live

Nickolas, you're my pride and joy
My precious baby boy
You're everything I prayed for
Nickolas, all my dreams are different now
You've got to me somehow
You're my miracle
You're my little miracle

There's nothing further I can say about what that boy means to me. Nick reinvented me the moment I held him close enough to hear his tiny heart beating in his chest. He rewired the circuitry of my brain and reworked the essence of my soul. He has never stopped pushing me--through the simple, sublime, ongoing miracle of his existence--to be a better man.

CHAPTER 29:
FOOL ME ONCE

A sense of humor is part of the art of leadership, of getting along with people, of getting things done — **Dwight D. Eisenhower**

* * *

In the summer of 1993, we had a steady stream of gigs coming our way and we'd started to earn a separate income making backing tracks. The opportunity to buy our first home in the UK arrived when we received word that our house in Durango had been sold. We didn't get much from the sale, but it was enough to cover the down payment on a house in the UK. My dad told us about a property he and his new wife had looked at in Bispham, so Anne and I went to see it for ourselves. It was a semi-detached house on Warbreck Drive with three small bedrooms and a quaint little back garden.

We immediately fell in love with it and closed on it as soon as we were able. We moved into the house just a few months before Nick was born and this was his home for the first 6 years of his life. All six of those splendid years were spent working hard and enjoying Nick's infancy and adolescence. NAP Music went from strength to strength, and its success led to me biting off slightly more than I could chew, in the form of a retail backing track store that I dubbed Track Attack. Not one of my better ideas, I don't mind telling you. I'll have more to say on Track Attack, and some of my other failed ventures, later on. Suffice to say, it was as unsuccessful as NAP was successful.

Life, back then, was all about Nick. Everything that we did, every effort and expenditure that we made, was entirely to do with putting food in his mouth and clothes on his back. Nothing else mattered to us. Any desire that we'd felt for wealth or fame vanished the moment he came into existence. Which is just as well, because both those things proved to be elusive to us, at least during the decade or so that followed his birth.

We kept gigging and touring around and did our best to bring Nick up right and steer NAP Music in the right direction. What a juggling act it all was. Our secret weapon, when it came to our own music career, was Ste. Having an extra pair of hands made all the difference––and his anarchic sense of humor didn't hurt, either. Life on the road only makes sense when you give yourself permission to laugh at the occasional unfairness and absurdity of it all. If Ste and I were to collaborate on a book focused solely on the stories we have from his time as our roadie, I can say without exaggeration that it would be twice the length of the one you're reading now! Two such stories, however, stick out for me.

Ste and I always used to take the piss out of each other at every opportunity. That was how we communicated. You always had to have your wits about you when Ste was the one dragging your gear around. This could sometimes be troublesome, but it helped me to stay sharp, even on days when my senses should have been dulled by hours upon hours of travel on little to no sleep. One time, he and I found that we had a little time to kill before a show, so we decided to play a quick game of pool. This was at a social club of some kind, which frequently had its own pool or snooker rooms. We used to play a lot of venues like that, but we seldom got to see what they had to offer. As Ste and I were wrapping up our game, shortly before our performance was slated to begin, he handed me his cue and said, quite casually, "go to the bartender and get the deposit back for the cues––I need the toilet." I thought nothing of this and promptly carried the cues over to the bar. It was a slightly odd formality, but my mind was already on the show that we were about to perform. I stood by the bar for some time, waiting to catch the bartender's attention, feeling the seconds tick by. Finally, I called the bartender over--I wasn't about to let a small deposit stop me from getting onstage at the appointed time. When I asked her for my deposit back, all I got in response was a confused stare. "Deposit? What deposit? We don't take deposits for the cues."

I'd been had. I turned around and saw him doubled over and cackling on the other side of the room. He got me good that time, the bastard. I made him the butt of the joke many times over the years, but in the final analysis, he probably got me twice as often as I got him. My favorite of his antics, by far, came not long after Nick was born. He couldn't have been more than 2 or 3 months old when it happened.

We were booked to play a social club in Wigan (and we made sure to double and triple check, this time, what sort of gig it was prior to showing up), and we had brought Nick along with us in his Moses basket. Ste, by this point, had become a combination roadie and nanny. He was whatever we needed him to be. One of his duties was to stay with Nick in the dressing room while the two of us were onstage. The ladies at this particular venue couldn't get enough of our adorable baby. They came flocking over to his basket from the moment we came through the front door. After the show, we were preparing to leave, and Ste went to pick up Nick's basket and carry it out to the van. Being the prankster that he is, however, he couldn't pass up the opportunity to have a little fun with Nick's adoring female fans.

He began by swinging the basket slowly as though he were rocking Nick to sleep. To help sell his deception, he looked down into the basket and spoke soothingly to its little occupant. All perfectly wholesome so far. But then, before a crowd of horrified onlookers, he started swinging the basket faster and faster, higher and higher. He looked like a homicidal lunatic––like he was about to hurl his defenseless infant charge onto the floor or into the ceiling at any second. This nerve-shredding charade went on for a minute or two before Anne emerged from the dressing room––with Nick in her arms. The basket was empty. Everyone either breathed a sigh of relief, or burst out laughing, or both. It was one of the funniest things I've ever witnessed. That was Ste's impish streak, in a nutshell. He was the sort of person who took one look at an empty basket and immediately asked himself what sort of havoc he could wreak with it. He may not have had a baby in that basket, but he did have that club in the palm of his hand. It was sheer chaos. Just the way he wanted it. I'll never forget the hilarity of that moment.

Anne and I, at this time, were in dire need of those kinds of good laughs. We were both stressed out––her more so than I, on account of the physical and mental toll the pregnancy had taken on her. She had gone back to work much too quickly after Nick was born. I wish I had talked her out of doing that. But we had to make ends meet, after all, and I suppose, after years of traveling and performing and scrambling about, we'd developed some unrealistic idea about our own stamina and the kind of abuse our minds and bodies could endure. We lacked the forethought to conserve our energy and take things slow. I consider us incredibly fortunate to have made it through that mad period in one piece. Having Nick made it immeasurably easier to keep going. And so did Ste, in his own way––at least when he was around, the madness was funny.

CHAPTER 30:
BAD IDEAS AND BOLD VISIONS

Success is no accident. It is hard work, perseverance, learning, studying,
sacrifice, and most of all, love of what you are doing or learning to do
—Pelé

* * *

When I reflect on the 1990s, it's not the gigs that tend to stick out. That was the decade when Anne and I became parents, and my memories of performing mostly get crowded out and shoved off to the side by my memories of Nick's formative years and developmental milestones. The best show of your life can't hold a candle to the sight of your son taking his first shaky steps. Still, there are a few career highlights I'd like to share.

We performed on Central Pier in Blackpool for the summer season of 1995. It was a comedy show, first and foremost, headlined by Mick Miller and featuring a new, up-and coming comedienne called Chrissy Rock. We were the only musical act. The show itself wasn't great, if I'm being honest, but it was a great learning experience for us, and primed us for what came next in ways we couldn't have predicted.

While the show wasn't great, Mick Miller was just brilliant – one of the best comedians we have ever shared the stage with! We got to know Mick quite well that summer, along with a slew of other UK comedy greats, like Johnny Casson, Jimmy Bright, Albi Senior and Paddy Greene.

Probably the highlight of our time in Blackpool, professionally speaking, was the summer season of 1998, when we played the Layton Institute. This was a step up from Central Pier, as far as we were concerned. The Layton Institute in Blackpool had hosted summer concerts for many years, drawing in enthusiastic crowds from across the region and beyond. These concerts were renowned for featuring top performers from various genres and disciplines. Comedy, music, theatre––the Layton Institute did it all.

It was a historic venue, the unique design and dimensions of which fostered an atmosphere of intimacy that allowed audiences to connect with performers on a personal level. The Layton Institute's annual summer season had been a staple of Blackpool's cultural scene for a long time before we came along.

Club blazes trail with fine show

THERE'S a certain irony in the fact that one of the best produced, fastest moving and most enjoyable summer shows in the resort isn't to be found on the end of a pier, won't break the bank for the price of a ticket and doesn't boast a single household name in its hard working cast.

While other venues have trimmed their entertainment stills or even, like Pelham Mount, vanished completely, Layton Institute still blazes a trail which must be the envy of many a mainstream theatre, let alone its fellow social clubs.

With the exception of the usual rota of comedians there's a whole new look and feel to this year's show. So while the posters still indicate a pecking order of performers, producers/directors Upstage Artistes and Productions have given A Night To Remember much more of an ensemble feel.

Gloss

Ostensibly, Big Big Talent Show finalist Nik Page is the bill topper but in reality focal duo Nu Attitude mould the proceedings together. Blackpool's Darren Coulton adds his own gloss and the new, young dance quartet Kikka add energy and more glamour.

There has a good strong clubland delivery and the image of a boyband member going it alone. His solo spot in the first half combines recent up tempo hits with more surprising items by Barry White and even Shirley Bassey.

Nu Attitude look and sound good with their James Bond medley and cleverly span the years from singalong on Spice Girls, proving melancholy at home with their first season at this venue.

Likewise Darren Coulton gets a first half about with On Broadway and Sunset Boulevarde's As If We Never Said Goodbye, both revealing his steady progress as a performer.

But it is the show's second half which is a standout with everyone coming together and all four vocalists throwing in everything and the kitchen sink (on selections, Elton John and Beatles medleys plus assorted other items) all accompanied by choreographer Kira Titterton's imaginative routines.

With such a closely knit production it's not easy for any visiting comedian to snugly fit into the show. Abi Senior seemed to sense this from the start, sounding oddly racy and taking longer than usual to find the flow of a routine which he has clearly tempered down from his more familiar blue one.

He's probably better than much of his material - there are some excellent moments as he capitalises on his girth and appearance but he lets himself down badly when relying on subversive racism and similarly sick throwaway lines.

Apart from that the whole thing could and should be put on the road once the season ends on October 31 to show what can be done in clubland.

ROBIN DUKE

When we were asked to co-produce and appear in the 1998 season, we were, quite naturally, thrilled. Gary Lawson (nickname "Mother") was the Music Director and co-producer. He and I spent hours and hours in the studio, building arrangements for the show and making the most of all the talent at our disposal. Only a couple of months before the show opened, Gary noticed a lump growing in his neck. It was concerning and so he wasted no time seeing the doctor and getting a prognosis. It was cancer and in the latter stages. He was given months to live and died the day after our opening night at The Layton. I didn't really know Gary that well, but I was proud of the show we put together and thought about him during every performance that summer. Our costars included Nik Page, Darren Coulton, and the dance group, Kikka. We are still friends with Nik and Darren to this day and chat frequently on Messenger or WhatsApp. In addition, each week, a visiting comedian came aboard to round out our ensemble.

Layton Institute 1998

The nonstop variety made it impossible to get bored, whether you were spectating or performing. It was a brilliant setup. We must have done around 125 shows that summer, and I'd be shocked if Ste and his wife Mel missed more than a dozen of them. They were a fixture of that whole summer season to almost the same extent that Anne and I were.

* * *

Nick was attending a private school in Blackpool, during this stretch of time.

He learned to play the piano there. His first recitals were, for me, the most enthralling, soul stirring musical performances under the sun. They spoke to and nurtured a deep part of my spirit. None of the musicians I shared the stage with at the Layton Institute had anything on that kid's rendition of "Chopsticks" and "Twinkle Twinkle Little Star"––not in this father's eyes, anyway. I never felt more like my beloved Uncle Harry than I did watching Nick play the piano for the first time. Somehow, I knew that he'd stick with music all his life and that a day would come when he'd have "MacArthur Park" in his back pocket, just like his old man.

* * *

As 1998 gave way to 1999, Anne and I knew that we were due for another shakeup. We sincerely loved our home country of England, but we had never stopped pining for the lifestyle and opportunities that America had to offer. We had only come back across the pond because we had desperately wanted a child––and now we had one. We both knew that the US was the country where we wanted Nick to one day spread his wings. Moving back was the right thing to do––for him, as much as for ourselves.

I knew we would be back in the USA by the time we got into the new millennium, so I think it was fitting, at least for me, that Manchester United saved their ultimate season as a backdrop for our last year in the UK. United had already won the Premier League title and the FA Cup by May of 1999 which meant that the elusive treble was a possibility if they could somehow beat Bayern Munich in the UEFA Champions League Final. Up until 1999, no team in history had ever won the treble.

The 1999 UEFA Champions League Final isn't just a memory for me; it's a heart-pounding journey that still sends shivers down my spine. As a lifelong Manchester United fan, that night at the Camp Nou stadium in Barcelona is etched into the very fabric of my being. From the moment the whistle blew, my heart was in my throat. Bayern Munich came at us like a tidal wave, and when they scored early, it felt like a dagger to the heart. But as a true Red Devil, I refused to lose hope. I knew that, with this United team, as long as there was time on the clock, anything was possible. Minutes turned into eternity, and with each passing second, the tension mounted. I watched through clenched fists as United fought tooth and nail and, truthfully, were definitely second best - until fate intervened.

In the dying moments of the match Teddy Sheringham poked home a mishit shot from Ryan Giggs. The stadium erupted in a chorus of cheers and tears. We were still in it, clinging to hope with every fiber of our being. I was behind that very goal – just 10 rows back – it was unbelievable.

But what happened next defies belief. As the clock ticked towards its final breath, Ole Gunnar Solskjaer etched his name into Manchester United folklore. His instinctive flick from David Beckham's corner and Teddy Sheringham's header sent the ball crashing into the net, and in an instant, our wildest dreams became reality. The scenes that followed are a blur of joy, disbelief, and unbridled passion. Strangers

142

embraced in sheer ecstasy, tears of joy mingling with sweat and rain. We had done it. Against all odds, against the relentless march of time, we had emerged victorious. The first person to call me after the match was none other than my arch-enemy (in football terms), but my best friend in life, my brother-in-law, Ste. Despite the fact that he would've hated United winning that match, he knew exactly what that win meant to me.

As I stumbled out of the stadium that night, my voice hoarse from screaming, my heart fit to burst with pride, I knew that I had witnessed something truly extraordinary. The 1999 UEFA Champions League Final wasn't just a football match; it was a testament to the power of belief, the strength of the human spirit, and the unbreakable bond between a team and its fans. And as a lifelong Manchester United fan, I wouldn't have missed it for the world and I will take that memory to my grave. As Sir Alex Ferguson said just minutes after the final whistle, "Football! Bloody Hell!"

* * *

Once we'd resolved to make the move happen, we put NAP Music and our house in Blackpool up for sale. It was risky, but we had cooled our heels for as long as we could, and we were ready for a new adventure. By the end of 1999, both our business and our house had been sold, and we had purchased our plane tickets back to America. The UK was the only home that Nick had ever known. We were leaving behind not only it but many of our closest friends and family members. But Anne and I felt stifled and burnt out, and we wanted Nick to have the best life we could possibly give him.

Selling off NAP enabled us to put a significant deposit down on a house. That was the first time in our lives that we had any serious money. This, in spite of the fact that Track Attack, my ill-advised backing track retail store, had been hemorrhaging money since we opened it. It only lasted about a year, so at least the scope of the damage was limited. I'd had the same goal in mind, when I came up with Track Attack, as I did when Anne and I hit upon the idea for NAP Music––to create a passive income stream, and to grow and flex my muscles as a businessman. It was a foolish idea, however. The business was so niche, and the pool of potential buyers was so small, that it didn't make any sense to operate a brick-and-mortar store. I think that having a physical storefront that I could point to had a certain grandeur to it--it made me feel like a proper business owner. The best thing I can say about Track Attack is that, while it was a financial drain, it didn't outright devastate us, and it didn't delay our return to the US.

My other unfortunate, unprofitable sideline, for a few years, around the turn of the millennium, was custom greeting cards. Anne and I had a go at that both in the UK and the US--and it went down in flames both times. We started by renting a unit in Botany Bay, a retail district between Blackpool and Manchester. Once again, my entrepreneurial spirit led me astray. I'd spent my whole life working for other people, and I thought it was high time I made something work for me, something that wouldn't require much from me, in terms of hands-on labor and supervision.

These entrepreneurial misfires taught me the importance of not overextending yourself and not trying to reinvent the wheel. I like to say that I learned that lesson right away, but as previously stated, I did try to open a second custom greeting card stall in a swap-meet after we got to back America. Anne was quicker on the uptake than I was. Time and again, over the years, she's had to disabuse me of my grand illusions. I'll come to her with some far-fetched idea, and she'll shake her head and say, "Nope, you've already tried that one, Terry. Do what you do – stick to what you know." Nobody can shoot me down as kindly as that woman can.

Saying goodbye to our family and friends--for the second time, at that--was one of the hardest things we've ever had to do. Moving away from Anne's family, in particular, created a painful rift. We had a going away party at the Royal British Legion, the working man's club in Netherton, close to their home and Bill's regular haunt. The occasion was touching but not without a certain amount of tension. Anne's dad was especially upset, and even a bit angry, that we were bidding all of them farewell. In fairness, we were taking his grandson away from him. He had a right to be cross with us, I think--but deep down, I believe he understood that the move would hugely benefit Nick. Thankfully, that minor undercurrent of strife is not my defining memory of that night, which was full of laughter, tears, and memories. Even the potential wedge that our decision drove between us and Anne's family didn't amount to very much in the end. We brought them over to visit us in the USA at least once a year from that point on. We saw more of each other than any of us had a right to expect that night in Netherton when we said our tearful goodbyes.

CHAPTER 31:
BACK IN THE USA

The secret to a rich life is to have more beginnings than endings
—Dave Weinbaum

* * *

After spending three cozy, if slightly cramped, months living with my Mum again, the itch to find a place of our own got to be more than Anne and I could bear. We'd heard good things about a place in Glendale called Arrowhead Ranch--a spot with a long, storied history, steeped in citrus farms, and, it seemed to us, palpably buzzing with the promise of community and serenity. Curiosity got the better of us, one sunny day, and we set off to see it for ourselves.

Driving through Arrowhead Ranch, that first day, basking in its golden mid-afternoon light, smelling its citrus trees, casting our eyes across its wide open spaces, made us both swoon. A sense of tranquility enveloped the whole area. It was easy to imagine Nick growing up there--and once we began imagining that, we felt a duty to make it happen. It seemed to us that we had stumbled upon a hidden gem of a place, a secluded and otherworldly glade, a region where the past and present blended together seamlessly. We couldn't picture a more perfect backdrop against which to write the next chapter of our lives.

We must have looked at a handful of houses, that day, and over the course of the next few weeks, each with its own charm, but nothing clicked until we stepped into one particular house on West McRae Way. Crossing the threshold for the first time felt correct to me in a way that I'm afraid I can't fully explain. It was like the opposite of a haunted house--a cheerful, sunlit place, eager to be occupied and brimming with promise and happy possibilities, rather than with restless ghosts. But it was supernatural, all the same. Every room, every window, every floorboard, whispered stories of future memories waiting to be made. I heard laughter echoing off the walls wherever I stood. Anne was every bit as enchanted as I was. We scarcely had to discuss it--we closed on it as soon as we could.

Settling into life at Arrowhead Ranch was like carving out a slice of Arizona paradise. The years that we spent there transformed us all, but none of us, unsurprisingly, went through a more dramatic transformation than Nick, who seemed to learn a hundred new things each day. That house was more than just a roof over our heads--it was the canvas upon which we painted our lives, a sanctuary where we grew like springtime shoots. Our neighbors were welcoming, our surroundings were beautiful. It was an ideal place to call home, and it felt to us like our humble abode on West McRae was the beating heart of it all.

Nick was just over six years of age, when we moved back--young enough to take big changes in stride, or so we hoped, but more than old enough to ask questions, and have preferences, and get homesick. Our first few weeks back in the US, we kept studying his reactions, looking for signs that we'd done the right thing, fearing we'd instead find evidence of discontentment. We moved into the new home we'd bought and enrolled him in Arrowhead Elementary School in Granada Hills. Anne and I used to go to the school playground when he was having recess and stand on the other side of the chain-link fence, watching him. We wanted to see for ourselves if he was acclimating to his new environment and getting along with the other kids. Our accents had been to our benefit when we'd toured the US--they had made us stand out from the competition in a positive way. But children can be cruel and quick to ostracize those who don't quite fit in for whatever superficial reason. Nick was the bedrock of our lives. If he wasn't happy and at ease in America, then none of us could be.

We were heartbroken when we saw that our son was all alone on the playground. He was standing apart from the other kids, not taking an interest in their games or mingling with them whatsoever. The other children didn't seem to be shunning him, as far as we could tell. He was the one who appeared to be keeping his distance. We started to ask ourselves whether Nick was shyer than we had ever realized, or whether the move had brought some latent shyness to the surface. He seemed to have no interest in approaching his classmates and making friends. As we watched him sitting on the swings by himself, he struck me as a lonely, isolated figure. It was a painful thing for a parent to witness. Anne started to cry. "Look at him," she said. "He's alone, he's not happy."

That afternoon, when he came home from school, we questioned him· "How are you liking your new school, Nick?"

"Oh, it's great, Dad. I'm loving it."

Gently and cautiously, we pressed him for details. Could it be possible that he was already mature enough, at the age of six, to make the conscious decision to conceal the truth from us so as to spare our feelings? Was he just putting on a brave face, so that we wouldn't worry about him?

I chose my next words carefully--I didn't want him to feel like he was being spied on. "Well, we swung by the school today, and noticed you're not playing with any of the kids."

He suddenly became more animated, and a smile spread over his face--a genuine smile. "No, because there's all these swings and slides and things, and I'm playing on them. All the things outside."

All at once, his self-imposed isolation made sense--the English schools he'd attended had abutted nothing but empty stone courtyards. There hadn't been any playground equipment. From Nick's perspective, the chance to swing and go down slides in the middle of a school day trumped the allure of social interaction––and as soon as Nick pointed that out to us, we understood it perfectly! What a relief that was. We were fretful parents who had forgotten how it feels to look at the world from a child's point of view. He wasn't lonely or unhappy in the slightest. On the contrary, he saw his new school as a marked upgrade––to his eyes, it was an amusement park! Once the novelty of those swings and slides wore off, we had no doubt he would start introducing himself to his classmates. But for the time being, friendship could wait. It didn't take him long to make friends, including his lifelong best friend, Jason Hayes.

They became friends in that first week at school and remain so to this day. Jason was a groomsman at Nick's wedding and those roles will be reversed this year at Jason's wedding. These are the very special things in life, for sure.

It reminded me of when my own family had moved from Openshaw to Glossop, when I had been about ten, and I had suddenly been shown a new world, a natural, green world, that I had never before imagined. Every epoch of my life has been marked by a move like that. Hearing Nick excitedly describe swinging and sliding to his heart's content made me think of all the time that my own view of the world had been expanded. I'd gone from Openshaw to Glossop, from England to Spain, from Spain to America––and each time, my conception of what life could be had deepened and broadened. It's so easy to lock yourself away, I think, in a small, black-and-white world, every last corner of which you know intimately. But you owe it to yourself to see what else is out there––to discover for yourself what it is you've been missing. When you're a child, of course, you lack the power to do so. Your parents take you here and there, as dictated by some combination of fate and necessity. But even then, sometimes you luck out. I knew that my boy would never forget his first week at Arrowhead Elementary, just as I have never forgotten the grassy hills and fields of Glossop.

CHAPTER 32:
JUST LIKE OLD TIMES

The only place where success comes before work is in the dictionary
—Vidal Sassoon

* * *

Our first big break of the twenty-first century, as musicians, came when we landed an ongoing job at a swanky venue in Phoenix, Arizona, called the Marco Polo Supper Club. It was the sort of establishment that made an immediate impression on patrons and performers alike. Situated in a narrow room with a stage at the far end, the club had a classy ambiance that made it a popular tourist destination as well as a favorite eatery of Phoenix locals. Its iconic avant-garde aesthetics and nightly live music were almost as big a draw as its extensive menu. The prices were not modest, but the food was gourmet, made from the finest ingredients, and the service and entertainment were likewise of first-rate quality. Anyone looking for a memorable and luxurious dining experience could find something to love about the place. When Anne and I played there, the head chef was Scott Tompkins. I don't care what part of the world you hail from, or where you've eaten--you have *never* tasted a steak as delicious as the ones aged and cooked by Chef Scott.

The Marco Polo was owned by the Mastro family, who went on to create a famous and profitable chain of steak and seafood restaurants. They were fantastic people to work for, with a clear-eyed understanding of what made a supper club commercially viable and appealing to customers. Live music was one of the main ingredients of Marco Polo's success. Talented musicians and singers performed there seven nights a week in a range of musical styles, including jazz, blues, and swing. A local musician, and good friend was the person responsible for getting us the gig at the Marco Polo. Pat Starke was a guitarist and ran his own cover band with his wife, Dianne Lindsay – The Dianne Lindsay Band. It's safe to say that Anne and I brought something a bit different to the table when we signed on. Her infectious, no-holds-barred personality won over the audience the very first weekend we played there. We were initially hired to perform on the "off nights"--that is to say, Sundays and Mondays. Those were, in theory, the quiet nights. But we did everything in our power to liven them up.

After two or three weeks of this, the general manager approached us one Monday evening with an offer. He wanted us to switch from playing off nights to a Tuesday–Saturday schedule--starting the very next night! We didn't hesitate to say yes. Those were the Marco Polo's busiest, liveliest nights. We always wanted to play to bigger, more energetic crowds. The more people who walk out the door humming your music, the better you feel. It had taken us just a couple of weeks to hit a home run. After that, we were back on our feet.

The older you get, the more you start to worry that you've lost your touch. It's especially difficult to get out from under that shadow when you're an entertainer who's not as young as he used to be. I was a father by this point in my life, but I still wanted my work to have the same vitality, freshness, and spontaneity that it had when I was in my teens and early twenties. Securing the Marco Polo gig and proving that we had what it took to dazzle a "main night" audience gave me just the boost I needed. I'm still touring to this very day--I can't imagine a day when I close up my piano and never lay my hands on the keys again.

I can't tell you how encouraging this promotion was for us at this point in our careers. Our professional life in America in the 1980s--before England, before IVF, before Nick--had been breathless, wide-ranging, and more than a bit mental, in hindsight. I accepted, when we decided to move back at the dawn of the 2000s, that we would probably not be able to just pick up right where we left off. America had not been on pause in our absence. Our chosen industry, and the culture at large, had changed. Many of the positions that we had once neatly slotted into no longer existed or had since been filled by someone else--someone younger, in a number of cases. In spite of all the time we'd spent in the US, we understood that we would be returning to it as strangers. We knew better than to expect otherwise.

Imagine our surprise, then, to say nothing of our happiness, when we went back on the road, and got a job offer from the powers that be at Red Lion--just like old times. We were amazed to discover that, while the crowds were no longer composed of the same people, they were still, in essence, unchanged. These people, flocking to the same venues we'd killed a decade earlier, still wanted to hear us play. It was the kind of warm welcome we had not dared to hope for. In the interest of turning back the clock as much as we could--and in the interest of catching up with an old friend--we dropped in on Jack Guier as soon as our Red Lion gigging took us back out his way. The usual pleasantries were all exactly as pleasant as you'd expect. "How are you doing, good to see you again," and so on.

But the real pleasure was introducing him to our son. Nick was a constant reminder that Anne and I hadn't actually managed to go back in time--but we were glad of that. He was also living proof of how much we had both grown.

On the last day of our stint in Washington, our van broke down. This was something it had been threatening to do for some time, so we were prepared for it psychologically, if not materially. It left us in a bit of a bind. We had the vehicle assessed and were told it was in need of a new transmission. I mentioned this irksome development to Jack in passing—forgetting, apparently, the sort of man he was—and he took charge of the situation straight away, which is an outcome I ought to have expected. He came to us later that same afternoon with a brand new SUV—a Chevy Suburban. It was a serious set of wheels. Spotless, never used. I looked at it in a state of total disbelief. The glint in his eye when I'd told him about our transmission trouble had told me that he was planning to spring some surprise on us, but I hadn't seen anything like this coming. I knew he had a kind heart and deep pockets, but I had figured that the most he would do—the most any reasonable person in his position could do—was pay for replacement parts so that our van could be patched up. But that was nowhere near generous enough for Jack.

"Jack, please, we can't. Where did you get this? How did you—"

"Think nothing of it. The car's brand new. I won't get any use out of it. Take it off my hands."

"We'll… we'll fix up the van, we'll find a way—"

"Oh no. Don't you worry about that. You're leaving the van with me. That SUV is yours."

We're talking about a $60,000 vehicle here. Once again, Jack had gone so far above and beyond on our behalf that words failed me. That's how he was. No strings attached, and no questions asked. He just stepped in and solved the problem. It's the same way I am now—thanks, in part, to his example. More than twenty years have passed since he gave us the keys to that beautiful Suburban, and I consider myself very lucky to be in the same position where I can help others in need. So I'm speaking from experience, having been on both sides of it, when I say that if you can afford to help your friends, then you should. It's never made any sense to me to hoard your money. I witnessed a lot of generosity growing up—but no single act of generosity will ever leave me as gobsmacked as Jack's decision to send us out of Washington in style.

CHAPTER 33:
PIE IN THE SKYE

Small opportunities are often the beginning of great enterprises
—Demosthenes

* * *

A lot of interesting characters came and went through the Marco Polo Supper Club when Anne and I worked there. The most noteworthy, for our purposes, was Ray McLeod, a Phoenix businessman and investor whose entrepreneurial ambition was the equal of my own (but whose instincts were definitely sharper than mine).

He used to grab drinks with Anne and I, from time to time, after our shows, or before we went on. Our conversations were rambling and discursive, but one subject that we kept returning to was the idea of opening a restaurant of our own. It seemed like little more than a pipe dream, at least to me, but it became increasingly clear that Ray was musing over the possibility more and more seriously as time went on. Every time we talked about it, we threw a little more fuel on the fire. We'd known him for about a year when he got to the point where that fire inside him could no longer be contained.

One night we were sitting on the patio at the Marco Polo, and Ray made it obvious that he was ready to get down to brass tacks. He asked us if we were serious about getting something off the ground. It was a bold question, but that boldness was exactly what Anne and I needed to see. Left to our devices, I think we might have kept idly daydreaming almost indefinitely. The Marco Polo was such a striking venue that it was easy to sit around, night after night, soaking up the atmosphere and fantasizing about the sort of place that you would like to run if you were a restaurateur. If we hadn't met Ray, that's probably as far as we would have ever gone--thanks to him, we went so much further. Ray was one of those guys who could make things happen, and he had a way of making you believe in yourself. He told us to draw up some plans and come to an agreement about exactly how we thought the place should look. I felt a bit of trepidation internally. Was this going to blow up in my face, like Track Attack and those damned greeting cards? But I didn't let my uncertainty stand in my way. We jumped at the chance that Ray presented to us. The following afternoon, the three of us met for lunch at the fish market in Scottsdale, and Anne and I scribbled a rough blueprint of our ideal restaurant on a napkin. We talked at length about the floor plan, menu, and overall vibe we wanted to create. From those modest beginnings, SKYE Restaurant was born. Sitting there in that fish market, looking at our amateur sketches but sensing what they had the potential to become, I felt like I'd been struck by a bolt of lightning like arcs of electricity were coursing their way down into my fingers and toes. Naturally, one of the first things we did was pull Chef Scott aside and ask him if he'd be interested in lending his considerable gifts to our cause. He had so much faith in what we were trying to put together that he became a key player on our core team and helped to conduct interviews in those crucial months leading up to our grand opening. He was an integral part of our ownership group, together with Ray McLeod, Jim Croft (another investor), and us two. All of us shared the same drive and the same commitment to boldness and quality.

Over the next few months, we worked tirelessly to flesh out our plans for SKYE. We scouted locations, conducted interviews, hashed out ideas, and put every leftover ounce of energy and passion that wasn't already going into our parenting or our music into making the restaurant a reality. The whole process was a roller coaster ride--the most frightening kind of roller coaster ride, where you're lurching from side to side hard enough to jostle the bones inside your body, and you're not totally confident that your restraints are secured correctly. At any moment, it felt like the whole thing could go completely off the rails, but despite that, we never lost sight of our shared vision. We scoured the city in search of the perfect location, debating and sizing up dozens of properties, ranging from rundown storefronts to fancy Scottsdale real estate, but nothing struck us as a good fit for what we had envisioned. If it didn't have that elusive "wow factor," something that made it stand apart from the pack, we knew it wouldn't stand a chance in the competitive world of fine dining that we were hoping to take by storm.

And then we found it. A plot of land in Peoria, at 83rd Ave and Bell, that was perfectly suited for our purposes. It was not only a prime location, but the property itself was spacious, with plenty of potential for growth. I stood on the sidewalk, taking it all in, and it was like I could see the sleek, modern structure in my mind's eye assembling itself before me as if my magic. The warm, inviting atmosphere of the dining room, the innovative menu, the live entertainment--all of these things seemed to be at my fingertips that day. It was as if I could will them into existence right then and there if I only wanted them badly enough. In retrospect, I can see that I was getting caught up in the excitement of the moment. The location wound up posing more challenges for the restaurant than we had anticipated. Peoria was still a growing city at the time, and it was not yet known for its culinary scene. We did not set out to be trailblazers. It just sort of happened that way. But that was what made SKYE so special--not only for us but for the community. It brought style to a part of town that was still in the process of forming its identity. In a sea of culinary mediocrity, it was an isolated island of high-class excellence. But I'm getting ahead of myself. First, we had to build the damn thing. And that building phase proved to be a grueling gauntlet of misfortune and unforeseeable disasters. Of course, I am telling this story from my sole perspective. There were so many incredible people involved at each stage, without whom SKYE would not have existed for certain.

One day in particular will be forever seared into my memory like a hot brand. We had invited Chef Scott Tompkins in as a part of the ownership group to join Ray McLeod, Jim Croft, and us two. We were in the midst of constructing SKYE, and things were proceeding smoothly--or so we thought.

The only snag we'd hit was a delayed shipment of steel roofing that we were supposed to have received from Texas. At that time, there was a massive steel short-age in the US. We made peace with the fact that we would have to wait, but we had no way of knowing just how long we'd be kept waiting. Three months crawled by as progress stalled, and everyone, from our builders to our investors to Anne and myself, became increasingly antsy. We had contractors and workers biding their time, and the steel shipment was nowhere in sight. Finally, we got the call--the steel had shown up, and everyone could resume work. We were all ecstatic as we watched the truck bearing the massive steel rods pull onto the construction site. There was a taco truck on the perimeter of the property, and we all gathered around it, sipping coffee, eating enchiladas, and watching the steel catch the sunlight. The mood was, at first, jubilant--but our excitement was cruelly extinguished when we saw that every last one of the steel rods was, for some unfathomable reason, cut three feet too short. Not one of them fit on the roof. They would all have to be replaced.

To this day, I don't know how it happened. It was such a humiliating, demor-alizing mishap, and it hit us like a punch in the gut. In an instant, we all went from feeling like kids on Christmas morning to feeling like mourners at a funeral. We had been waiting far too long already for that damned steel, and we were now being made to start the wait over again from the beginning in the middle of a nationwide shortage. That appalling setback cost us six months--and we knew that there was a high likelihood of that six-month delay becoming a death sentence for SKYE if our funds were to run out in the interim. But we were determined to make it work. We regrouped, we rallied, and we kept pushing forward. SKYE was our future, no matter what--but that day, our future did not look bright.

CHAPTER 34:
THE GRAND OPENING

In the end, it's not the years in your life that count. It's the life in your years
—Abraham Lincoln

* * *

About three months before SKYE was due to open its doors to the public, we started scouting for staff members to join our team. We knew that we needed the best of the best--people who were passionate, skilled, and possessed the ability as well as the willingness to dazzle our patrons. There were so many amazing people vying for a spot on our staff, and choosing between them was no easy feat. Eventually we settled on a group that we felt embodied the spirit of SKYE. After that came weeks of training and preparation. By the time SKYE opened for business in 2006, we knew in our hearts that everyone we'd hired to work there understood our vision and wanted to help bring it to life. Two of those important additions were Eric Bennett and Tanya Queen. Eric came with a wealth of experience as a General manager and Tanya was (and is) simply the best private event specialist in the industry. We worked side by side for the first few years at Skye, and she was brilliant!

I can still tap into the feeling of nervous excitement I felt that day we opened. Some remnant of it is still rattling around inside my psyche after all this time. My mind was beset by uncertainty and a slew of anxious questions. Would people like the food and the music? Would they enjoy themselves, and tell their friends, and keep coming back? I knew that these questions would not all be answered by the end of our first day or even our first week. That sort of suspense is an unavoidable part of the experience of owning your own business. If you have one or more failed businesses under your belt, as I do, you can't help but be a little wary and distrustful of your own enthusiasm. I'd gone into Track Attack with high hopes, only to have those hopes dashed when it became apparent that it was shaping up to be a money pit. The sting of that disappointment sticks with you and colors every subsequent risk that you take as a businessman. During the first few months that SKYE operated, there were many encouraging signs, but it wasn't always easy to take them at face value and breathe a sigh of relief. I kept waiting for a sudden downturn, for interest to wane and the crowds to thin. But the longer I waited, the clearer it became that my worries were unfounded. I didn't have a dud on my hands this time – together with others, we had created a thriving business and an establishment of which I am intensely proud.

Over the next seven years, SKYE became a beloved fixture of the community, a haven for foodies and music aficionados alike. People came from all over the valley to dine under our roof, watch our shows, and experience the singular magic that only we were offering. We slaved over that place, both before and after opening day, putting in the extra effort to refine and optimize its every minute detail. When I think back on this period of time and remember all the work I put in to make SKYE what I wanted and needed it to be, I feel a great swell of pride, both for myself and every staff member. I can say, without a doubt, that I did everything in my power to make that place the best version of itself. I only wish that I could say the same about my relationship with Anne––it pains me to admit that I cannot.

Anne and I were starting to drift apart while all of this was going on, and I accept *all* of the blame for that. I was so preoccupied with running SKYE that I had begun to neglect her. It took me too long to admit to myself that the business had gone from a shared dream of ours to a wedge that was being driven between us. This was a sobering realization. Some nights, standing in our restaurant, with servers and diners milling about me and the clamor of conversation and clinking silverware filling the air, I thought about the hasty doodle that Anne and I had drawn on that napkin and tried to picture myself hemmed in by its crude, straggly lines. Even when looking at the woodwork and stonework of the finished structure, I could see our original harebrained vision underpinning every last girder and floor tile. No one else––not the servers, not the musicians, not the patrons––could have possibly seen what I was seeing. No one, that is, but Anne. It breaks my heart to realize that I had alienated her so much that she was not able to truly partake in that glory with me. I knew that I had to make amends. Our dream was taking flight––and I refused to let either of us be left behind on the ground.

I am unutterably grateful that Anne and I were able to pull through that rough patch and that it is now a distant memory, bearing no resemblance to the life that we now enjoy. SKYE was a testament to the fact that anything is possible if you aim high and apply yourself, but it was also a massive strain on my personal life. My memories of SKYE continue to inspire me, but Anne has been, and will always be, the primary source of inspiration in my life. Our relationship, like SKYE, is nothing if not a monument to big dreams. I knew that I had to get us back on course, no matter what. None of my successes––in the realm of business or anywhere else––would mean anything to me if she wasn't around to help me celebrate them.

As far as SKYE was concerned, our celebrations were somewhat short-lived. We had been open for about two years when, in 2008, the economy crashed, creating a destructive ripple effect throughout the fine dining industry. Our restaurant was not spared. One of the primary effects of the recession, the consequences of which we started feeling almost immediately, was a decline in consumer spending as people became more cautious with their finances. Practically overnight, we saw a massive decrease in customer traffic. And it wasn't just average consumers that we started to see less and less of. Corporate dining, too, dropped off significantly as many companies began scaling back their expenses and looking for ways to cut corners. One of the first things they put on the chopping block was meals and entertainment for their employees and clients. That might have helped their bottom line, but it hurt ours severely. This decline in corporate clientele dealt a death blow to many fine dining establishments as we made our way through 2008 to 2009 and beyond. At SKYE, the corporate drop was over 80%. We had been dealt a grievous wound, and all that we could do was hope against hope that it would not prove fatal.

The precariousness of our business and our lives had skyrocketed from one day to the next due to factors that were well beyond our control. In the wake of the crash, I observed a pronounced shift in consumer preferences that did not bode well for SKYE's chances in the long term. The average American, after 2008, had to make do with a tighter budget. Recreational spending went way down, and the demand for "fast casual" dining experiences increased. I took the lay of the land and noted what our competitors were doing to adapt to this changing landscape. Many fine dining restaurants were forced to introduce prix-fixe menus and special promotions to coax cost-conscious consumers back through their doors. I was willing to do whatever it took to ensure SKYE's survival, but my hunch was that its salvation would have to come from the entertainment side of the operation. Given that I have a background in music and the mind of a performer, it's perhaps unsurprising that I felt that way.

We needed to invent a new reason for customers to visit SKYE. If we couldn't lure back our old clientele, we'd have to cultivate a new one. I didn't know just how we were going to pull it off. I just knew that we had to make it happen somehow. I turned the problem over in my head continuously as our bills mounted and our prospects dimmed. But it was Anne whose idea ultimately saved the day.

CHAPTER 35:
HAVING THE TIME OF YOUR LIFE

Failure is not an option

—Gene Krantz

* * *

AbbaFab 2008

Prior to the economic crash of 2008, our weekends at SKYE were pure magic. The energy was consistently high and the vibes were unfailingly cheerful, with the crowd dancing the night away to a mix of current hits and beloved tunes from the 1980s and 1990s. It only took us a few weeks of operation to figure out that, when it came to getting everyone out of their chairs and onto their feet, nothing did the trick quite like ABBA. Their songs always seemed to cast a spell over people.

As soon as the iconic opening notes of "Dancing Queen" hit the air, the dance floor would instantly fill up, transforming in a matter of seconds into a bustling party zone. It was like clockwork, the way every occupant of the restaurant would simultaneously fall under the sway of a single unified rhythm. Even our patrons who weren't big on dancing couldn't resist tapping their shoes to the beat. That was the seed from which Anne's stroke of inspiration sprouted.

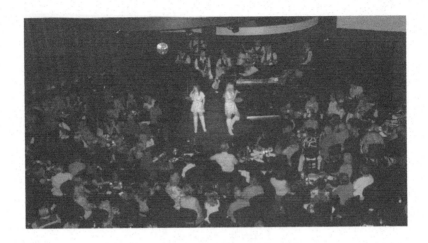

She proposed the idea that would ultimately save SKYE off the cuff, one fateful afternoon during a leisurely brunch. We'd both been trying to come to terms with the restaurant's impending doom and racking our brains for the solution to our money troubles. The jeopardy that SKYE was in was by no means unique, and there was no particular reason that we should stay above water while so many other eateries sank. But SKYE was special to us––we'd imagined it together––and we were not about to let it go without a fight. She got a distant look in her eyes that day at brunch, thought for a moment, and then said, in a casual tone of voice that belied the importance of the idea she'd just hit upon: "Why don't we go all-out with costumes and put on an ABBA tribute show?"

I knew at once that she was onto something. It was a way to generate renewed enthusiasm for the restaurant without taking on any significant new expenses. In the short term, it would improve our chances and give us a concrete task to focus on instead of engaging in helpless, unproductive fretting. In the long term, it would evolve into something more robust and remarkable than either of us could have predicted.

From that initial spark, "ABBAFab" was born. But that was only the beginning. What started out as a recurring tribute show structured around the music and style of ABBA gradually grew, against all odds, into an entertainment and booking agency that came to be known, in time, as TAD Management.

I've already gone into a few of my ill-judged business ventures, in addition to touching on NAP Music, which was a standout success. Looking back over my

162

career, I think it's fair to say that, out of all the ideas that Anne and I hatched, all the companies that we got up and running, there were two that really had legs, two that made us feel as though we'd struck gold. NAP Music was the first. TAD Management was the second. In between the two came SKYE, which was a more qualified success, but one that's still worth celebrating now—and was still worth fighting for, back in the day. SKYE was shaped, in large part, by the business principles that I picked up from conversing with Ray McCleod, and in many respects, it served as a blueprint for TAD later on when it began taking shape. I wouldn't have made half of the good decisions I made with TAD if I hadn't taken in and absorbed the business lessons taught to me by Ray McLeod. It was a valuable learning experience as well as a labor of love. That's why I felt so strongly about keeping it afloat in spite of the recession. ABBA was to be our lifeline and the answer to our prayers.

ABBAFab was far from the only new addition that Anne and I entertained, but it was the one that had the most merit, as far as we could see. Our menu also saw a fair number of shakeups and slashed prices—no one on the west side of town could justify paying $45 for a steak anymore, no matter how delicious it was. But we knew that merely reducing the cost of our entrees and appetizers wasn't going to get the job done. If we had only implemented that change and no others, we would have risked signaling to our customers that we had only transitioned to providing an inferior, albeit more affordable, experience. We didn't want to do anything that would connote cheapness in their minds. The trick was to pair reduced prices with some perk, some service that we had never offered before, thereby creating an unmistakable value proposition. To get patrons coming through our door in droves, we would have to take a big swing, risk looking foolish, cross our fingers, and hope that it all paid off. For Anne and I, two lifelong performers with a history of throwing caution to the wind and rushing headlong into uncharted territory, such gambles come naturally.

As a professional musician who has evolved, over the course of many decades into a business owner and talent manager, I've been well-positioned to observe the shifts in consumer preferences that have sculpted the music industry. I've seen niche markets explode, without warning, into the mainstream, and I've seen popular markets dwindle into borderline nonexistence. There isn't much rhyme or reason to any of this, but if you can sense which way the wind's blowing, or if you just happen to get lucky, then you'll make money hand over fist. Believe me when I say that tribute bands are a much safer and stabler venture now than they were in 2008. Because they weren't all the rage back then, starting ABBAFab felt exciting and unfamiliar for us, as well as for our audience. We were really just flying by the seats of our pants. Top to bottom, the whole thing was a bit ramshackle and thrown together, especially at the beginning. But Anne's natural flair for commanding the stage pulled all the disparate pieces together and made the whole production work better than it had any right to. She was always the secret ingredient.

We had no clue how our tribute show would be received or if anyone would even bother buying tickets. Anne and I were straying well outside our comfort zone. We'd done covers in the past but had always tried to put our own stamp on them. Rigorously recreating another artist's look and sound as faithfully as possible had never been in our wheelhouse. But we took a leap of faith and put two shows on sale--one for Friday and another for Saturday. If it proved to be a disaster, at least it would be confined to a single weekend. The first heartening sign came straight away when both shows sold out in the blink of an eye.

We reacted first with disbelief, followed by a wave of relief. Suddenly we had people eagerly shelling out $20 apiece just to walk through the door to our restaurant on a weekend evening, most of whom would be sitting down and grabbing a bite to eat while they were at it. Money was changing hands twice. This had the immediate effect of making us feel more financially secure, but it also meant that the pressure was on to provide a top-shelf entertainment experience that would justify the increased cost of entry.

If the crowd reactions and ticket sales are any indication, then we held up our end of that bargain. The show sold out again and again, and the energy in the Platinum Room was consistently off the charts. Somehow, in the midst of the 2008 economic downturn, we had stumbled onto a winner. ABBA perfected the art of feel-good pop music, and for that reason, their songs were the perfect musical accompaniment for us in that moment of triumph. We had made the best of a bad situation, and the air buzzed with the joy of that improbable victory every time we took to the stage in our flamboyant ABBA attire. We knew that our struggles were not yet over, but nevertheless, we were conscious of the fact that we were faring better than many other businesses in our same position--and that we still had a fighting chance.

CHAPTER 36:
AN UNLIKELY IDOL

Your talent is God's gift to you. What you do with it is your gift back to God
—Leo Buscaglia

* * *

After selling out twenty or so ABBAFab shows, one after another, we started to ask ourselves how we were going to keep things varied and maintain our momentum. Even ABBA's impeccable tunes would start to get stale after a while if they were all we were doing. The natural follow-up was to branch out into experimenting with other tribute bands. Anne and I surveyed our decades of performing and took stock of where our own musical strengths resided in an effort to determine what else we could bring to the table. Two names presented themselves to me immediately, two artists whose respective sounds perfectly complemented one another: Elton John and Billy Joel. It was a complete no-brainer. I had incorporated a ton of their songs into my repertoire years prior when Anne and I had toured as a duo, and I still had a good handle on many of them. As we desperately needed an influx of cash, it's perhaps no surprise that my mind wandered to the artist whose signature song had once compelled legions of inebriated strangers to "put bread in my jar" night after night after night. With the same talented band from ABBAFab by our side, we got to work on crafting a sturdy, crowd-pleasing setlist with a good mix of Billy Joel and

Elton John. By late 2008, not long after the initial debut of ABBAFab, our "Piano Man" tribute was ready for its turn in the spotlight.

The trickiest part was maneuvering the grand piano from its usual place within the restaurant onto the stage in the Platinum Room. That alone would have been a logistical nightmare––now consider that we somehow had to squeeze it onstage alongside a 10-piece band. I have no idea how the staff was able to pull off that particular miracle. They did a fair bit of grumbling about it, but I can't say that I blame them. ABBAFab shows weren't without their own headaches, but compared to the Piano Man shows, they were a walk in the park. The people who worked under me at SKYE naturally shared my commitment to keeping the restaurant open for business––but when they realized that a Piano Man show wouldn't be complete without, you guessed it, a piano, they didn't exactly jump for joy.

All of that extra grunt work was revealed to have been worth it, however, when Piano Man made its big debut. The enthusiasm with which our new show was met was every bit as full-throated and infectious as that which had greeted our ABBAFab gigs. We kicked off with classics like "Bennie and the Jets" and "The Ballad of Billy the Kid" and kept the audience hooked right up until the final note of "Piano Man." That first Elton and Billy show gave us all the assurance we could have possibly needed that we were not just a one-trick pony, as a tribute act. The path to SKYE's salvation had seemed frightfully narrow at first––but it was widening steadily with each new addition we made to our roster of tribute shows. I'm proud of everyone at SKYE who labored tirelessly and went far beyond the usual duties of a restaurant employee to make those weekend concerts the crowd-pleasers that they were. The price that I must now pay is that, to this day, I can't catch up with any of them on Facebook without being subjected to good-natured ribbing about all the times they had to "move that damn piano!"

ABBAFab and its ilk weren't the only things we were doing to enliven SKYE and offer enticement to new and returning customers. We also began hosting a talent competition that we dubbed "Idol in the SKYE." Tribute shows were far from a safe bet back in those days. Anne and I knew that we were taking a big swing the first time we tried to put our stamp on "Dancing Queen." The same cannot be said for Idol in the SKYE. Talent competitions were all the rage during that era due to smash-hit reality TV shows like *American Idol* and *America's Got Talent*. We knew that if we played our cards right, Idol in the SKYE could be a major coup for us, a surefire money maker as well as an ongoing source of both surface-level entertainment and engrossing, unvarnished real-life drama. It was all that and more. One unexpected moment of synergy that arose from it came when a talented young contestant named Chelsea Faulds impressed us so much that she secured a spot for herself in the very first cast of ABBAFab. We had accidentally invented a talent competition that doubled as an audition process for our tribute bands. It blew our minds to see firsthand how much talent there was waiting to be discovered in the greater Phoenix area.

Perhaps the contestant with the most talent--and certainly the one with the most dramatic story, the details of which were unknown to us for quite some time--was a woman named Charity Lockhart. We knew as little about her as any of her competitors when she first walked through the door to our restaurant. She was a woman in her mid-30s who didn't originally hail from Arizona. That was about the extent of our knowledge, initially. All we needed to know, in our capacity as judges, was whether she could sing.

She settled that question definitively the first time she got onstage, delivering a heart-rending, soulful rendition of "Somewhere Over the Rainbow" and handily wiping the floor with the competition. Her abilities carried her all the way to the finals. I could see that she was determined to come out on top, and I dimly sensed that she probably needed the winnings more than most, if not all, of the other singers that she was up against. Anne and I sympathized with her instinctively. We were no strangers to hardship ourselves. After all, we had initiated Idol in the SKYE, ABBAFab, and all of our other schemes in a desperate bid to keep the restaurant open. But we were, at that point in our lives, as it happens, very far removed from the sort of dire straits in which Charity had found herself.

What we did not know--what we did not learn until after the competition came to a close--was that Charity was a victim of domestic abuse who had escaped her abuser and fled south from Detroit with her two young children in tow. The three of them were living out of her car, which was parked in SKYE's parking lot. Anne and I were astonished to discover that Charity was taking the small sums of cash she won from her Idol in the SKYE performances, going outside, walking a few hundred yards, and bedding down for the night in her vehicle alongside her kids. Her mettle was as awe-inspiring as her voice––but her voice was all that we had access to for the duration of the competition. And it was more than enough.

Charity won Idol in the SKYE, the year that she competed––and, with all due respect to the other contestants, she all but walked away with it. I believe she earned a little over a thousand dollars, all told. In less capable hands, this would not have been a large enough amount to last all that long or yield meaningful change. But it was enough for her to put a deposit on an apartment and extricate herself and her children from the mess they'd been forced to endure. Never again would any of them spend a night sleeping in their car.

We lost touch with her for a period of several years. We hoped, all the while, that she was continuing to make use of her considerable talents and pursuing her singing career––a hope that was rewarded, finally, when she emerged from the woodwork in 2018 and pitched us on a Whitney Houston tribute show. We countered by asking her to audition for the cruise line that we were gigging for at the time, which she did. I needn't tell you that she knocked them dead, the same way she did to everyone who had the privilege of hearing her sing "Somewhere Over the Rainbow," the first time she set foot in SKYE. She's now a prominent headliner in the cruise industry and has been enjoying a fantastic, lucrative, and rewarding life for years. Hers is the greatest underdog story to which I've ever personally borne witness––and I couldn't be happier to have played an instrumental role in it.

CHAPTER 37:
TURNING POINT

Don't try to make a million pounds.
Just make one pound and do it a million times
—**Thomas Stroud (my grandfather)**

* * *

We fought like hell to keep our restaurant's doors open and its lights on. It was a bitter fight, at times, but we also relished much of it. Sinking our teeth into the songs of ABBA, Billy Joel, Elton John, and a whole host of other sensational artists made the struggle so much sweeter and more satisfying than if we had only been slashing prices and offering promotional deals in order to keep ourselves afloat. I have become a shrewder businessman as i've aged, but deep down, I'll always be a musician first and foremost.

Unfortunately, the ravages of the 2008 crash eventually proved to be more than our business model could bear. All of our scheming and brainstorming, no matter how inspired, could only forestall the inevitable for so long. When SKYE closed its doors and switched off its lights for the final time, in 2012, it felt like our whole world was crumbling around us. It was wonderful while it lasted.

We immediately flew into damage control mode. We had lost our livelihood, and we could not afford to rest on our laurels while deliberating endlessly about our next move. At the same time, we did not want to leap into action without any kind of strategy. We found ourselves huddled at a table in a Starbucks, sipping coffee and weighing our options. The prospect of returning to the road life we'd once led--spending countless hours performing in bars and lounges, 4 to 6 nights a week--was daunting and unappealing. We were in our fifties, and I couldn't see that being a sensible long-term decision for us. And even if we'd had the stamina for it, our earnings wouldn't have come close to replacing the income stream that we'd lost when SKYE went under. It would have been akin to slapping a Band-Aid over a grievous, gaping wound. We did not want to settle on a disagreeable short-term fix and tell ourselves, *well, it's good enough for now*, only to then become trapped in it. Life has taught me that you can talk yourself into almost anything, so long as you can convince yourself that it's only temporary. *Good enough for now* is, in its own way, a dangerous line of thinking.

It was a scary time, to say the least. But we knew that we still had each other. That was the one constant in our lives, whenever the going got tough––that, and our beloved son, Nick, who we were also counting on to rise to the occasion. We walked into that Starbucks with no firm game plan, knowing that we needed to settle on one before we walked back out. That lunch turned out to be every bit as pivotal for us as the one that had birthed SKYE. We tossed around several ideas that day, but there was one that we kept circling back to, one that we had bandied about at various points in the past: setting up our own booking agency and production company. This time, with our backs against the wall, we resolved to really make it happen and to do it right. I wanted to keep applying the lessons I'd learned from Ray McLeod but to push further and aim higher. His understanding of the broader entertainment industry was somewhat limited, and I didn't want to be constrained by any limitations any-more––be they his or my own. Anne and I made a pact then and there in that coffee shop: if we were going to do this, it would be on our own terms. No more dancing to someone else's tune. Every success or failure would be ours to own. High risk, high reward. If we came out on top, we'd be the ones who reaped the benefits. And if we crashed and burned, then it would be us, and nobody else, who paid the piper.

With that, TAD Management was officially born. Terry and Anne Davies–– "TAD" for short. It was the start of an incredible journey, a breathless sprint down a road that curved and twisted and surprised us at every turn. We already had a few successful, established tribute shows at our disposal––ABBAFab, Piano Man, The Magic of Manilow, The 3 International Tenors––along with a few bands that we had brought in from California to perform at SKYE, including Bella Donna, Queen Nation, and Turn the Page. Several of these acts had already garnered a good deal of attention and fostered small but loyal followings in Arizona. The thing to do, now that SKYE was a thing of the past was to aggressively branch out, spreading our talent around and expanding our bookings into more local venues. Casinos, it seemed to me, were a logical first step. Once we started to make inroads in Arizona's casinos and performing arts centers, things really started to pick up steam.

One of the opportunities that came our way that seemed rather inauspicious at first glance ultimately became one of our greatest triumphs. It came about after we received an invitation to view a showcase at Sun Village, courtesy of Adrienne Miller, a booker we had previously collaborated with. Adrienne had always been a supporter of Anne and I, so we jumped at the chance. It was at that showcase that we crossed paths with Sandy West, a regional activity manager for a chain of RV resorts catering to snowbirds fleeing their chilly northern climates. These resorts, frequented primarily by Americans and Canadians over 55, were hemorrhaging money with their concerts, Sandy confided in us, in spite of the range of shows they offered.

Sensing untapped potential, I pitched Sandy on an ambitious but, it seemed to me, well-reasoned plan: a complete overhaul of their concert infrastructure, resulting in a shift in focus towards tribute bands, with the occasional national act. On the surface, it seemed like a gamble, and perhaps even an unwise one, by certain objective metrics, but inwardly, I have to say, I didn't feel that way about it. If I'm being perfectly honest, I didn't consider it a gamble at all. I had seen what tribute shows had done for SKYE's business--I had seen them making a profit during a time when it seemed that nothing else could--and I knew that the people who populated Sandy's resorts belonged to roughly the same demographic that had supported and enjoyed ABBAFab and Piano Man.

Sandy decided to proceed with my plan. Thankfully, my confidence in it was not misplaced. In the first year alone, after the restructuring, we managed to turn a sobering $250,000 loss into a $100,000 profit for her RV resorts. To this day, they remain one of our most cherished clients and a testament to the power of fearless innovation. You have to be willing to seize opportunities when they arise and not let past failures or missteps rattle you. If you see a sure thing when everyone else just sees a risk, then you owe it to yourself to go for it--because no one else will.

Fate seemed to be smiling down on us all through TAD's whirlwind first year. Not only did we change Sandy's fortunes for the better, but we also gained a valuable addition to our team in the form of Adrienne Miller, the same person who had invited us to the showcase at Sun Village. With Adrienne onboard, we set up shop in a cozy office in Sun City and got to work expanding TAD's reach. We were soon joined by Cindy Brock, who we had worked with when she was an activity director at one of the over-55 communities. Our expansion was faster and more far-reaching than we had dared to dream it would be. I love Cindy! She is still with us at TAD and, in many ways, a big reason for our success.

By 2015, TAD Management had improbably become the undisputed heavyweight champion of resort entertainment in Arizona, representing over 50 tribute bands. We had cemented our reputation and laid the foundation for a lasting legacy. That alone was a reason to celebrate--but our future was even brighter than we knew.

CHAPTER 38:
SONGS AT SEA

Change is inevitable and constant. It's important to anticipate and adapt to it rather than resist it (Who Moved My Cheese) —**Spencer Johnson**

* * *

In the early days of TAD, the scope of our operation was fairly limited. Of course, it makes sense to start small, when you're getting a new business up and running, but it wasn't mere practicality that kept me from dreaming bigger. The simple fact of the matter is that I wasn't aware of all of the options available to me. There were so many potential avenues of profit of which I was completely ignorant. The cruise ship industry was one of many things that wasn't anywhere on my radar. I had no conception of its significance in the world of entertainment. So when Linda Raff called us out of the blue one day, on behalf of Bramson Entertainment in New York, and offered me and the rest of ABBAFab a job aboard a Holland America ship, doing our tribute show for a leg of a world cruise, I didn't know quite what to think. It sounded too good to be true, but I had little to no frame of reference for what it would actually entail. I reasoned that, at worst, it would be a somewhat more glamorous version of the sort of gig work that Anne and I had done for decades. Working aboard cruise ships actually proved to be rather closer to working at the Belplaya in Spain--they're nothing so much as seaworthy luxury hotels, awash in tropical sunlight, packed full of cheerful vacationers, abuzz with live music and memories in the making.

I took Linda up on her unexpected offer, and four weeks later, Anne, Chelsea Faulds, Scotty Pearson, and I found ourselves on a plane to Chile, where we would be boarding a Holland America cruise ship bound for Papeete, Tahiti. I was so bowled over the first time I set foot on that ship--so enamored with the grandness of the vessel and the dazzling expanses of sea and sky that lay beyond it--that I found myself waiting for the other shoe to drop. But as it turns out, there was no catch. It was precisely what it looked like--precisely what I wanted it to be. I can point to a small handful of moments in my life when I knew that everything had changed for me. Boarding that ship was one such moment. As I walked the ship's deck and felt it rising and falling gently with the waves, it was as though I could detect a paradigm shift in my own perspective happening beneath my very feet. I knew, after just a matter of days at sea, that I had found something that my life would have been incomplete without.

Anne and I had never been on a ship of that caliber before, and we truly didn't know what to expect or how to comport ourselves. We didn't know how to dress, where to go, or what the audiences would be like--that first day, in particular, we hardly even knew which way was up. It was all very alien to us. And as if the ship itself weren't foreign enough, it would also be taking us to parts of the world that we had never seen before. Before we departed from Chile, all of us went out on the town, and Scotty, being the most adventurous member of our group, ordered ceviche, which made him sick as a dog. The poor man spent his first four days at sea in quarantine, alone and violently ill. I remember that first cruise as a magical, eye-opening experience, and I like to think that Scotty would agree in spite of how much of it he spent throwing up in his sequestered cabin. You have to take the bad with the good, I suppose when you're exploring the unknown.

ABBAFab was by no means the only band that had been contracted to perform aboard that particular leg of Holland America's world cruise. The ship was swarming with talented musicians and other performers, taking in the sights and mingling with the other passengers, though I doubt any of them were as mesmerized by their surroundings as we were. Because we were far from the only game in town, there was plenty of downtime. Our first performance wasn't until five or six nights into the cruise, though we did rehearse with the ship's resident band beforehand. We went on and absolutely killed it. The audience ate it up. Doing justice to ABBA's timeless, indestructible tunes thrilled us as much as it did them. The entire crossing took the better part of two weeks, consisting almost entirely of sea days––a planned stopover at Easter Island was scuppered on short notice on account of rough weather, which saddened us––and in all that time, we only did two shows. This meant that we had lots of time to luxuriate and get to know our fellow travelers, the professional entertainers and the vacationers alike. A few chance encounters still linger in my memory.

We came upon a group of retirees one morning out on the ship's deck. 65 and up, mostly, all of them cruising around the world. One of the group's most aged members engaged us in conversation. She made quite an impression––she was 92 years old, still had her wits about her, and knew the ship better than most if not all of its own crew members.

I remember seeing her walking around on Deck 3––walking around faster than anybody else, might I add––and looking leftward and rightward, like she owned the place and loved every inch of it, like its every bolt and bulkhead had met with her approval prior to its installation. And she had every right to feel a certain sense of pride. As I got to know her, we learned that she lived on the ship nine months out of the year, and had done so for the last twenty years. Cruising was her life. "I have four kids," she explained to us, "and I like three of them. So every year I spend a month each with the ones that I like, and the rest of the time I'm at sea." I couldn't have asked for a better traveling companion to introduce us to the world of cruising. She was so unbelievably buoyant but also prone to bouts of fussiness and quick to tell less experienced cruisers than herself--everyone, in other words--where they were and weren't allowed to go and what they were and weren't permitted to do. Everyone took heed when she issued these instructions, as though she were at the very top of the ship's chain of command. She was an extraordinary and unforgettable old lady--and incredibly, I'm told that she only just passed away within the last year or so. I can only hope, for her sake, that she was breathing salty sea air when it happened.

You come across the most colorful characters out on the high seas. People you've never met before but with whom you quickly establish deep and lasting connections. And you never know when a cruise might see fit to spring an unforeseen reunion upon you, as well. Shortly after Anne and I boarded that first Holland America ship, we were roaming around and familiarizing ourselves with the layout of the hallways below deck, and Anne rounded a corner and almost literally bumped into Nik Page, with whom we'd performed at the Layton Institute 15 years earlier.

Talk about a sight for sore eyes. The memories of that summer season and the strong camaraderie we'd formed with our fellow entertainers there came crashing back over us in an instant. Quite an odd feeling to play a bunch of gigs with someone in Blackpool, lose touch with them for over a decade, and then reconnect with them just off the coast of Peru!

CHAPTER 39:
NATURE'S WRATH

You realize that life is fragile, and the most important thing is to do what you love while you can — **Miranda July**

* * *

Disembarking in Tahiti, I was suddenly struck--not for the first time, nor the last--by the sheer improbability of my own path through life. How had that kid from Openshaw found his way here? What on earth had he been doing on that luxury cruise ship? How had he found his way to the sandy beaches of that coastal hotel, the powdery slopes of that ski lodge, and everywhere else he'd been? He had no business being in any of those places, surely. And yet, there I was. It was sure as hell a gentler and more enjoyable jaunt across the water than what I'd been able to afford, back when Anne and I had braved the Bay of Biscay. I've actually come to enjoy going through rough weather aboard cruise ships in recent years, because you can detect how the vessels are handling the chop, compensating for all the dips and rises, smoothly navigating the sorts of waves that had mercilessly pummeled that Spanish car ferry. Nonetheless, I retain a healthy respect for the sea and its inconceivable power. Any seafaring individual, no matter what kind of craft they're in, must remain humble and vigilant and never forget what the ocean is capable of. To do so is to court disaster. This underlying wariness helped to countervail my disappointment when the elements conspired to stop us from landing at Easter Island. A few tenders managed to make it ashore the following morning, but it was frightening to watch them struggle to return to the ship over the churning waters. As badly as I wanted to see Easter Island up close, I can remember feeling glad that I was where I was, and not where they were. An even more terrifying reminder of the ocean's capriciousness and its capacity for destruction, loomed up before our disbelieving eyes one day as we were exploring Tahiti in an episode that almost deprived us of Scotty, our good friend and guitarist, forever.

We had come to a rocky, windswept cliffside, in the course of exploring the island. The preceding hours had been a paradisial procession of azure waters and lush landscapes, and we were totally at ease. But our sense of calm was about to be shattered in the most awful and sudden fashion. Scottie, ever the adventurer, had picked his way closer to the edge of the cliff than the rest of us. If another minute or two had passed without incident, it's entirely possible that we would have ventured further out ourselves and joined him. I cannot say for sure what would have become of us if we had. In any case, we hung back, about 300 yards off, long enough for the danger to reveal itself--after which point I was unable to move, unable to assist Scotty in any way, unable to do anything but yell out to him, to scream at him to run for his life. A titanic wave--a frothing wall of water--rose up from the seemingly serene coastline and crashed, with a booming impact, over the cliffs upon which Scotty was standing. It was an absolute monster. As it dashed itself upon the bluff and broke apart, sending torrents of water cascading in every direction, we lost sight of Scotty--and I, for one, sincerely feared that I had seen the last of him. When the waters receded, I thought that they would take him with them--wash him away, like some lightweight splinter of driftwood, some insignificant bit of jetsam. Our cries of horror turned to relieved gasps as we made out Scotty clinging for dear life to the craggy ground as the retreating wave sucked at his limbs and his clothes.

Scotty did not relinquish his grip upon the slippery cliffside. The wave rolled back--but he remained. He'd been battered and scared out of his wits, but he was alive. As if his brush with spoiled ceviche hadn't been punishment enough for his hubris and his adventuresome spirit on that trip--the poor guy just couldn't catch a break.

Colossal rogue waves weren't the only hazards we had to be on the lookout for, during those first several years of cruise work. We did over 50 engagements with Holland America, and in the process we explored the globe, anchoring every-where from Norway to Sweden, to Denmark, to Estonia, to Russia, to Portugal, to Iceland--the list goes on and on. I think being inundated with this torrent of exotic locales caused me to lose perspective and let my guard down somewhat. That's the only way I can explain how I responded the day I got a call from an agent based in Florida who asked me if we'd like to book an engagement with Disney Cruise Line. My better judgment ought to have kicked in, but I'm afraid that it failed me. I had a huge soft spot for Disney, so perhaps I was predisposed to jump on the deal unthinkingly. There wouldn't have been any issue with this offer--it was a perfectly legitimate one--were it not for one small detail that I had chosen to overlook in my haste: it hadn't come from our agent. Instead, it had come from a competitor. In a moment of pure naivete, I rang up Linda at Bramson to share the good news with her. She was, as you'd expect, less than thrilled. Not long after, I got a follow-up call from Jan Stenning, one of Bramson's agents, and a heated discussion ensued. I would say that it stopped just short of being an argument. But it all ended amicably enough.

Cooler heads prevailed before any bridges were burned. Jan and I both saw reason, and I accepted that I, in my ignorance, had nearly been successfully poached--not an uncommon pitfall in that industry. I reaffirmed my loyalty to Bramson. Just a few days later, we received our first contract with Disney Cruise Line. Jan had come through for us. She's highly respected within the industry and with good reason. Little did I know that my rather contentious phone call with her, foreshadowed future developments in our professional relationship--developments that would dramatically alter the course of both our lives.

It's a good thing that the Disney offer came through when it did. The cruise industry can be highly fickle, and windows of opportunities for those who perform aboard cruise ships are often more fleeting than they first appear. Our tribute act was the "flavor of the month" for a good three or so years with Holland America--a pretty good run, by the standards of this crazy line of work. We saw parts of the world we'd only dreamt of, thanks to those Holland America gigs, but it was only a matter of time before we moved on to try other things. I say that without any bitterness--I'm thankful for every one of those Holland America engagements. Playing music aboard cruise ships is really not unlike taking a vacation. You sing twice a week, for under an hour each time, and that's it, you've earned your keep. It's a frankly outrageous way to make a living--and I'm eternally grateful that we stumbled into it!

CHAPTER 40:
FATHOMS BELOW

All our dreams can come true, if we have the courage to pursue them
—Walt Disney

* * *

Being hired by Disney represented for us, among other things, an opportunity to rethink our approach to the art of the musical tribute. When we'd done ABBAFab for Holland America, there had always just been four of us, standing in for the two lead girls and the two main guys in ABBA, and we'd been supplemented by the house band. When our first Disney cruise rolled around, we were joined by Mike on drums, and by our son Nick, and therefore came aboard as a sextet--no house band accompaniment necessary. I wanted us to become more self-sufficient, and less reliant on strangers since we weren't familiar with Disney's operation and didn't know quite what to expect. As it turns out, my wariness was fully warranted.

We boarded our first Disney cruise in Stavanger, Norway. Right away ill omens abounded. The ship had come over from Canada and had passed through weeks of terrible weather that had prevented it from anchoring at its scheduled stops in Greenland and Iceland. And, to top it all off, it was raining in Norway. The passengers were, perhaps rightfully, pissed off. We knew we'd be playing to a prickly, hostile audience but also to an audience that was eager for any kind of relief--our success was by no means assured, but neither was our failure.

If I'm not mistaken, we were one of the first--if not the very first--tribute acts that Disney ever booked aboard one of their cruise ships. In that sense, Disney was straying even further outside of its usual wheelhouse than we were--though that didn't do much to allay my nervousness. A staff member approached us, as we were preparing for our first performance, and said to us, "Look, these passengers have had a rough go of it so far, is there any chance you could do your set out by the pool?" Eager to please our new employer and quite ignorant of the pain in the ass that we were creating for ourselves, we agreed to this unconventional arrangement. A poolside show would allow our listeners to recreate in two ways at once--the better to mollify them, we reckoned, after their cramped and unglamorous crossing. It was only after we moved up onto the deck, situated our gear beside the pool, and began bombarding the ship's crew with questions that we realized what a potential nightmare we had blundered into. The crew on the Disney ships were brilliant, and between us we quickly realized that they were not prepared for a band with a drummer!

Live bands with drummers were a foreign concept, aboard Disney ships. They dispatched a few members of the entertainment crew to descend into the bowels of the vessel and dig through old storage rooms, in the vain hope that they might chance upon what we needed. They finally unearthed a cobwebby drum kit from an old Disney jazz band that had played the ship in some bygone era. They dragged it up onto the deck, and we dusted it off and tried our damndest to see the humor in the situation. We managed to play our first Disney gig outside, however, the rain started up again shortly after we started, sending all the passengers scrambling indoors. There hadn't been very many of them to begin with.

Our next show took place in a proper venue—The Disney Theatre. They'd directed us to do a show onstage in the main theatre, a space that usually played host to scaled-down versions of Disney's Broadway hits, such as *Beauty and the Beast* and *The Lion King*. What we offered was quite the contrast with our Abba show--and I think the audience took notice of that and appreciated it if the response we got from them was anything to go by. That show was a big success!

Thus began three remarkable years with Disney. Nick, being a massive Disney fan, was in seventh heaven. His fondness for all things Disney actually wound up saving us from a rather funny predicament one night during the course of one of the first Disney cruise engagements. This is another story that I never tire of telling. We were scheduled to do a show in a lounge called Fathoms on board the ship. It was a small place that catered mainly to adults and held about 250 people at most. We'd been making a big splash with ABBAFab and we were contracted, for our second show, to mix things up with our tribute to Billy Joel and Elton John, Piano Man. It was the edgier of the two shows, and that's why we were debuting it at Fathoms. We thought it would be a good fit--that is, until the curtains rose, and we saw 100 or more kids crowding around the edge of the stage, with their adult guardians mingling with one another further back, beyond the reach of the stage lights. A sudden rush of panic gave us all a simultaneous jolt. Nervous glances were quickly exchanged between us as we launched into our first song. We all knew what was coming. The second song on our setlist was "The Bitch Is Back"--we can't do *that* song in front of a bunch of kids on a Disney ship! But what else could we do? The setlist was pre-planned.

And here we have an outstanding example of Nick's ad-libbing skills. He turned to me, just after our first song ended, with its final note still hanging in the air, and said, "I've got this, let me introduce the next song, I'll sing it, trust me." He had a glint in his eye and a smirk on his face that told me that whatever wild improvisation he'd devised was already making him laugh internally, and he had absolute confidence that it would go over well with the crowd. I didn't stand in his way. Nick strode forward, turned on the charm, and started putting in the work to get our unexpectedly youthful audience members jazzed up.

"Hey kids, how're you doing? Is everybody having a good time? We're gonna do a song for you right now--uh, your parents might know it as something a little different, but that's okay--we're gonna do 'Stitch Is Back!' Hit it!"

He did the whole thing in Stitch's voice. It was an inspired choice. The kids went wild for it. We were all so convulsed with laughter. At the same time, somewhere underneath the mirth, I felt a wellspring of pride. One of Nick's strong points onstage is that he's so quick and funny. He's refined that skill to the point where it's practically his trademark It used to be that you never quite knew what was going to come out of his mouth, but his instincts have only become sharper with the passage of time. That night in Fathoms has to rank among his crowning achievements. "Stitch Is Back!"--I just couldn't believe my ears. A good thing, I'd say, that he just so happened to already have that impression in his back pocket.

CHAPTER 41:
AN UNEXPECTED ACQUISITION

*The biggest risk is not taking any risk. In a world that's changing really
quickly, the only strategy that is guaranteed to fail is not taking risks*
—Mark Zuckerberg

* * *

I count myself as awfully lucky when I reflect on the fact that my working relationship with Jan Stenning might not have survived another agent's attempt to poach me
away from Bramson. If our paths had diverged there, I would have been robbed of
an industrious and shrewd agent whose labors did a lot to push TAD Management's
Cruise Division in the right direction.

We were represented by Bramson, an entertainment company in New York
City, and Jan was one of the agents there. Initially, we were working solely with Linda
Raff, but slowly, Jan began working directly with us. She continued to book ABBAFab
and Piano Man aboard cruise ships for the next several years, and we steadily became
friendlier and better acquainted. After a time, we grew close enough that she began to
confide in me her plans to leave Bramson in the not-too-distant future. She'd been in
the cruise industry for more than 30 years, at that point in her life, and was looking
to get out of it. Not wanting to lose her talents or her friendship, I told her that she
should consider coming to work for us, if and when she wound up splitting from
Bramson. TAD was growing exponentially, and I knew she'd be a stellar addition to
our team if her goal wasn't to retire outright.

I'd estimate these conversations of ours went on for about six months, at odd
intervals. Every now and then she'd reaffirm that her days at Bramson were num-
bered, and I'd hastily remind her that TAD wanted to scoop her up the moment her
services became available. I used to joke with her––though there was a good deal of
truth in it––that I had a proposal for her all written up that I was ready to press send
on at a moment's notice, just as soon as I got word that she was quitting. Finally, the
long-awaited day came. "I've made up my mind," she said. "So, do you want to talk?"

Of course, she already knew my answer. Anne and I met with her, and the three of us hashed out the details over lunch, which took no longer than an hour or two. She found our terms agreeable and told us that she would give notice and jump ship--so to speak--the following day.

The next morning, I got a call from Linda. The instant I heard her voice, I bristled in anticipation of the reaming I was about to receive. But she took a different tack entirely and caught me totally by surprise. "Look," she said, "Jan's great, we're not happy that she's leaving us, but there's no hard feelings, I understand how she feels. I want out too. I'm not going to keep doing this on my own, I'm too old. Do you have any interest in buying Bramson?" I really didn't have any interest in buying another agency, so I told her I was luke warm on the idea but would give it some thought.

The conversation could have quite easily ended then and there. But strangely enough, it didn't. That was only the beginning of our negotiations. Linda knew that it would be nigh impossible for her to fill Jan's shoes, and she was determined not to be saddled with a talent agency that she could not run effectively. What she wanted was money--more money than I was willing, or able, to part with. Eventually, she and I were able to formulate a plan that would span a period of about three years, after which we would own Bramson. I remember traveling to Spain for a cruise with AbbaFab while all of this was still up in the air and finding myself back in the airport in Malaga--the very airport where Anne and I first met. In the minutes leading up to our departure, we worked with Linda and our contract attorney in a bid to iron out any wrinkles before inking the final version of the deal. We were slated to board a cruise ship in Gibraltar, and we wanted to have everything settled before we did so, since the wifi on board, even on the ritziest ships, is reliably lousy. So that's what we did – in the space of a few weeks, TAD had gotten a whole lot bigger.

This was a pivotal moment in the history of TAD, a moment that, in many ways, propelled us into the big leagues. We left that airport feeling as though we'd been launched out of a catapult or fired out of a cannon. Such a strange sort of cosmic coincidence that our lives would be profoundly changed for a second time in the same concourse where we'd first laid eyes on each other. And that was not the end of our trip down memory lane. As we drove from Malaga to Gibraltar, we passed by towns and landmarks that we had left our stamp on together when we'd been young. Torremolinos, Marbella, Puerto Banus… it was as potently surreal as it was synergistic. It was like we were being treated to a highlight reel of our early friendship and courtship, curated by fate itself, in order to help us commemorate our crowning achievement as business people, and reflect on just how far we'd come.

That's how TAD's cruise division came into existence. We picked up where Linda left off and took it from there. At the outset, our primary goal was just to try not to mess anything up. Jan was an invaluable aid when it came to that. She knew the cruise business better than anyone. In the middle of 2024, she made the decision to retire after 40 years in the industry – some achievement! The cruise division has grown by leaps and bounds, thanks to her skillful stewardship, under our watchful eye and with the help of a fantastic team.

The idea of acquiring Bramson would have never occurred to me if Linda hadn't pitched me on it. There was something about her proposal that felt oddly fortuitous and made a bizarre kind of sense to me. It could have easily turned into an unmitigated disaster for all involved, but I think it was a win-win for everyone in the end. Linda might have been furious with me for luring Jan away. We all came together and settled on a solution that left everybody feeling satisfied.

From our humble beginnings as a two-person operation in 2012, to our acquisition of Bramson in 2016, and up to the present day, TAD Management has matured into something that has outstripped my wildest dreams. In little more than a decade, we've expanded our team to over 30 full and part-time staff, with offices spanning from Phoenix, to Fort Lauderdale, to Orlando, to the UK, to Dubai. And our journey is far from over––we're in the process of opening an Australian office as I write this. Internally, we refer to ourselves as the "TAD family," and we treat each other accordingly. Treating people well is at the core of everything we do. Not everyone I've hired has been a good fit for the organic culture that we've cultivated, but all businesses inevitably must go through those sorts of identity crises and growing pains. In my capacity as CEO, I've made a point of doing my damndest to provide opportunities for everyone who answers to me. My mission is to expand TAD while approaching every professional interaction with a spirit of fairness and mutual respect. While we've had to navigate some choppy seas, we've never run aground. I intend to keep it that way for a long time to come. TAD's best days are still ahead.

CHAPTER 42:
CITY OF GOLD

Dubai is a melting pot of cultures, a city of tolerance, where the future meets the past —**Sheikh Mohammed bin Rashid Al Maktoum**

* * *

The ongoing success of TAD Management has carried me forward to the present moment. There have been ups and downs, but as I get older, it seems that the highs get higher and the lows are no longer as low as they used to be – and that's how you hope they stay. I almost don't know what to make of it. It's so unlike the life I had as a boy and a young man. But I don't want to make it sound as though I've lost my wanderlust and my youthful passions entirely. I still spend much of my time on the road, playing shows and meeting new people––you'll have to pry my piano keys from my cold, dead hands. And even when I do stop for a spell and put my feet up, the place where I usually do so is a bit unconventional.

Sometimes we meet people after shows and get to talking about our lives. Oftentimes they'll ask us where we call home when we're not on tour. When we tell them that we live in Dubai, we tend to be met with surprise, skepticism and raised eyebrows. "Why Dubai?" they ask. You'd think we'd replied that we live on the far side of Venus. What I tell them, by way of explanation, is that I've seen huge swathes of the world, and Dubai is the safest, cleanest, and all-around best city I've ever lived in, a place seemingly devoid of political unpleasantness and religious enmity. And a place, in fairness, that I myself had never considered living in until a combination of a momentary whim and simple happenstance brought me there in 2019.

I was just off the shores of Japan, performing on a cruise ship, and Anne was at our niece Hayley's wedding bachelorette party in Tenerife, in the Canary Islands. Hayley's wedding was to be held in Liverpool in a few week's time. When my stint aboard the ship ended, I wound up in Hong Kong. Anne and I are no strangers to feelings of displacement, disorientation, and jetlag, but our experiences have taught us that these sensations are a lot easier to grapple with when we're together. Our objective was to rendezvous first before trekking back to Liverpool. How we went about that was up to us. We had thousands of miles to traverse, and about a week and change to kill.

Anne flew halfway across the world to meet me in Hong Kong. Initially, the plan was to spend a leisurely week there and then fly back to the UK for the wedding. I rather liked what I saw of Hong Kong, but Anne couldn't stand it there. Not wanting to subject her to an extended stay in a city that she loathed, I did what I had always done, whenever we'd found ourselves turned around and stranded somewhere back in our gig days––I consulted a map. We literally eyeballed the distance from Hong Kong to Liverpool and picked a destination that was on the way, roughly halfway between point A and point B. It's not that we'd never heard of Dubai prior to this silly exercise, but we'd never thought of it as a vacation destination. "Let's go to Dubai," I said. "Why not?" I looked up some outgoing flights from Hong Kong, and we were off.

For the next four days we stayed on Palm Jumeirah, a man-made island close to Dubai Marina, immersing ourselves in the extravagant opulence of Dubai––the "bling," as it's often called. We saw the Burj Khalifa, the Dubai Marina, a dizzying slew of beaches and restaurants, and all the other eye-catching locales that we could squeeze into our time there. It was incredible, but it was very much a vacation. We were thinking and acting like tourists, not like prospective buyers or renters. That changed on our second trip, which came after the wedding of Anne's niece––and after the advent of COVID.

During the pandemic, the United Arab Emirates was the first country to start lifting restrictions on Americans being able to fly. As you might expect, these flights were very inexpensive. Like everyone else in that troubled time of lockdowns and social distancing, we were crawling up the walls and anxious to reinject some variety into our lives. The reduced cost of the plane tickets alone would not have been enough to tempt us––but our pleasant memories of that four-day stopover in Dubai gave us all the additional incentive we could have possibly needed. Anne and I flew back out there, accompanied by Nick and his wife Julia, and rented a condo on the 27th floor of Marina Gate II. This was prime real estate, with a spectacular view of the gulf's warm, inviting waters and the marina's glittering, majestic skyline. We stayed for two and a half weeks. This was a long enough stay for us to acquire a deeper appreciation of the local culture than what we had initially come away with, our first time in Dubai.

Initially, we went into it with the same tourist mindset, talking up this or that glitzy attraction to Nick and Julia. "You gotta come see this, we've gotta go there," etc. But then, bit by bit, a strange thing began to occur. The longer I strolled Dubai's streets, the more I started to feel at home in them.

I remember sitting in a Starbucks in Dubai Marina Mall and observing two things back to back that had the effect of shifting something inside me. First, I happened to notice that one of the tables near me was unoccupied, but that its prior occupant had left his wallet, laptop, and phone behind. They were sitting out, in plain view, in an outdoor seating area, for about an hour before he returned to collect them. He had gone off shopping and had apparently thought nothing of leaving his valuables behind. I couldn't understand what I was seeing. But that is by no means an uncommon occurrence in Dubai. Nobody steals there. They simply don't steal. It brought me great peace of mind to know that I didn't have to watch my back, as I got my bearings, and that I never had to worry about being robbed or conned.

The second thing I noticed was, if anything, even more oddly utopian. As I sat in that Starbucks, waiting for Anne to finish her shopping, I saw little kids of varying ethnicities and religious creeds playing together in the street. Their carefree frolicking reminded me of my own childhood games and my far-fetched footballer dreams, though my friend groups in Openshaw and Glossop had not been anywhere near as diverse as theirs were. A feeling of serenity settled over me. *This is how it should be,* I thought to myself. *This would be a nice place to live.*

So, we started doing some research before that second Dubai trip had even ended. Anne and I vacationed there again about eight months later. By that point, we had begun seriously entertaining the idea of settling down there. We were fortunate enough, thanks to the success of TAD, to be in a position where we could afford to entertain such ideas. One misconception about Dubai that I'd like to clear up, having said that, is that it's wildly expensive. People see the superficial bling and assume that everything must be overpriced and that the culture must be steeped in rampant consumerism. It actually costs far less to live there, I've found, than it does to live in most of the other countries where I've pitched my tent. And while the bling is good for impressing visitors from out of town, it's not what really attracted us there and keeps us there. We're far more drawn to the melting pot aspect of the place, the distinct lack of politics and to the vision that Dubai has for itself.

10 Myths about life in Dubai

MYTH: YOU MUST BE ABLE TO SPEAK ARABIC **FACT:** Arabic proficiency isn't a necessity for living in Dubai. While it's admirable to learn the language, most people get by just fine with English. Even in professional settings like British International Schools, English is the lingua franca, making Arabic fluency optional.

MYTH: YOU CANNOT BUY OR CONSUME PORK **FACT:** Despite common belief, pork is available in Dubai, albeit in limited places like designated supermarket sections and select restaurants. Establishments such as Spinneys and Waitrose stock pork products, and certain dining spots like McGettigans' cater to pork enthusiasts.

MYTH: YOU CANNOT BUY ALCOHOL **FACT:** Contrary to popular misconception, alcohol is obtainable in Dubai, though not as openly as in some other places. Specialty shops like African and Eastern, and restaurants attached to licensed hotels, offer alcoholic beverages. Recent law changes have also simplified alcohol consumption regulations.

MYTH: DUBAI IS UNSAFE **FACT:** This is a massive misconception! Despite its Middle Eastern location, Dubai is recognized as one of the safest cities globally. The low crime rate and strong security measures contribute to a sense of safety, allowing residents to feel comfortable leaving belongings unattended even in public spaces.

MYTH: WOMEN MUST ALWAYS BE COVERED **FACT:** While respecting local customs is important, there's no strict mandate for women to be fully covered at all times in Dubai. Modest attire is encouraged, especially in religious sites and during Ramadan, but the city's dress code is more relaxed than commonly assumed.

MYTH: YOU CANNOT WEAR A BIKINI **FACT:** Beachwear is perfectly acceptable on Dubai's beaches, given the scorching climate. However, modesty is appreciated when transitioning from public beaches to other areas, requiring a cover-up like a t-shirt. This applies to all genders for respectful public appearance.

MYTH: YOU HAVE NO RIGHTS **FACT:** Dubai has robust laws and regulations safeguarding residents' rights. Individuals have successfully challenged companies in court, highlighting the legal protections in place, particularly in areas concerning work and labor rights.

MYTH: EVERYONE IN THE UAE IS WEALTHY **FACT:** While the UAE boasts its share of affluent individuals, the majority of its population comprises hardworking expats in various sectors. Income disparities are significant, with many residents earning modest wages and living in shared accommodations.

MYTH: DUBAI IS A CONCRETE JUNGLE **FACT:** Dubai's landscape isn't just skyscrapers; it features ample green spaces like parks and gardens, alongside ongoing initiatives for eco-friendly urban development. Beaches and desert landscapes add natural beauty to the city's modern skyline.

MYTH: THE UAE'S WEALTH IS ONLY DUE TO OIL **FACT:** While oil historically fueled the UAE's economy, significant diversification efforts have led to a thriving economy with sectors like tourism, finance, and real estate playing pivotal roles. Today, oil contributes only a fraction to the country's GDP, showcasing its economic resilience and adaptability.

Fatefully enough, we wound up buying an apartment situated above the one we first rented in Marina Gate II, with the same floor plan, albeit nearly 20 stories further up. The view is even more spectacular than before––but the most alluring thing that we can glimpse from our window is not the waves or the skyscrapers, but rather a hazy dream coming into focus, an aspirational goal, the promise of a future Dubai that is still in the act of coming into being. That is more precious to us than gold

CHAPTER 43:
UNDER THE KNIFE

The greatest wealth is health
—**Virgil**

* * *

Making a home for ourselves in Dubai solidified the sneaking suspicion I'd had for many years that my loved ones and I had escaped the pull of poverty once and for all. It was a force that had been acting upon me my entire life, like a kind of gravity, yanking me back down to earth every time I seemed to be on the verge of taking flight. It's not that my life is free of obligations now, far from it—-the runaway success of TAD and its subsequent expansion brought all sorts of new responsibilities into my life. But I'm able to stay atop them rather than being crushed beneath them.

Dramatic weight fluctuations have been an issue for me ever since I entered my thirties. The culprit is simple enough: I love food too much! After I turned thirty, my relationship with food became increasingly volatile and informed by emotional eating and other unhealthy habits. I consoled myself, at first, with the knowledge that I seemed to be able to lose pounds almost as quickly as I gained them. But my fluctuating weight was taking a toll on my system—-and the periods of weight loss were never commensurate with the periods of weight gain. I was steadily trending upwards. Food was a source of comfort for me, but it was also, I began to realize, a major weakness—-and it would have been my downfall had I let it.

In my twenties, I'd always gotten plenty of exercise. That, in tandem with my youthful metabolism, had kept my weight in check. Staying fit came to me so naturally, for so many years, that I started to let complacency set in—-and the older you get, the less complacent you can afford to be, where dieting and exercise are concerned. As life got busier and more complex, the numbers on the scale continued to climb higher and higher.

The SKYE chapter of my life was when my weight started ballooning badly. SKYE was a confluence of incredible stress and delicious food, which proved to be a catastrophic combination for me. I stood in the midst of that perfect storm all through the recession, over-indulging in order to keep my worries at bay whenever it seemed like we were about to have to close our doors for good. I have no one to blame for this but myself and my own lack of discipline. Before I knew it, I was weighing in at over 260 pounds. Then 280. Then 300. But I brushed off these warning signs and stuck to my bad habits. Even after SKYE went bust, things didn't improve much. TAD is a more successful and less stressful operation than SKYE ever was, but my outsized appetites had been firmly established by that point. I was set in my ways, and it was all too easy not to practice self-control amid my lifestyle of nonstop travel and burgeoning success.

This, of course, could only end one way. On my 64th birthday in 2023, I steeled myself, stepped onto the bathroom scale, and was greeted with a horrific sight. I had climbed to 365 pounds. That was when the worries that had been murmuring at the back of my mind for years became a clamoring choir of panicked voices. My blood pressure was sky-high, and I was even beginning to have difficulty walking. I had let things get out of hand, and the situation had become urgent. My knees were on the verge of giving in, and I knew that basic walking and normal functionality would soon be beyond me if I didn't shape up. Just a few months prior to this birthday, we went on a family trip to Disney World in Orlando, Florida and I spent 5 of the 6 days getting around on a mobility scooter. Of course, we had some laughs with that, but it was starting to play on my mind.

The time had quite obviously come to do something--but what? I had avoided the issue for so long by then that it was second nature for me to leave it on the back burner until a "better time" came along, a time when it felt right to finally set aside the energy and summon the willpower to address it. I was, of course, deluding myself-- that perfectly opportune moment never would have materialized. The best I could hope for was an intercession by someone who could perceive the damage I was doing to myself and the danger I was in, both of which I refused to acknowledge--someone who was in a position to fix what I had broken. That was what happened during an otherwise routine doctor's visit the year after we moved to Dubai.

195

It was Anne's doctor, not my own, that came to my rescue. She asked him if he could consult with me about my weight. In broaching the subject with him, unpremeditatedly, she was only doing what any concerned partner would have done--but she could not have picked a better person to ask. He told us that his colleague and best friend was one of the world's leading gastric surgeons and asked me if I would like to speak with him--not by appointment, at some future date, but right then and there. This distinguished colleague of his worked just down the hall. Five minutes later, I was sitting in his office, getting an earful about gastric bypass surgery, which was something I had never seriously considered prior to that day. But I had put myself in a position where drastic measures were called for. I was scared of what might become of me if I didn't take immediate action. After spending 15 minutes learning about the procedure in this doctor's office, followed by a brief talk with Anne, I was ready to take the plunge. There were attendant risks of which I was made aware. But nothing could have been riskier, I am certain, than continuing to put on weight the way I was.

Brace yourself for the best part of this story--the part that never fails to elicit flabbergasted expressions whenever I tell it in person. The conversation that culminated in me agreeing to go under the knife took place at 2:30 on a Wednesday afternoon. I told this doctor that I wanted to be officially marked as a candidate for surgery. I went on to explain that I was going to be in Dubai for the next three months, and it was my hope that he could squeeze me in somewhere in that timeframe. His response to this was, "What are you doing this Friday?"

I honestly thought he was joking. He was not! There had to be a catch, surely. Maybe it was the cost? Nope. It was $10,000 altogether, which included not only the surgery but also the hospital stay and 12 months of aftercare appointments. Unbelievable--and one of the reasons I love the United Arab Emirates!

Less than 48 hours after that impromptu meeting, I was in King's College Hospital in Dubai, being prepped for gastric bypass surgery. Two days after that, I was back in my apartment in Marina Gate II. It was nothing short of incredible. Everything that was happening to me seemed to be sped up, as though I were fast-forwarding through the entire ordeal––even my recovery, the part of the process I had dreaded the most, was surprisingly quick and relatively painless. After three weeks of eating nothing but plain yogurt, jelly, and broth, I went back to the doctor's office to be weighed. Glancing down at the scales and seeing a 28-pound loss cheered me just as much as the sight of the number 360 had frightened me on my birthday. My eating habits now bear little resemblance to those that got me into all that trouble–– my appetite has been dramatically curtailed.

Ten months after the surgery, I was down to 260 pounds. 100 pounds had simply fallen off me. And that was just the beginning of my weight loss journey, which continues to this day. It was a life-changing––and, I have reason to believe, life-extending––experience, one that I seriously doubt would have ever fallen into my lap if I hadn't relocated to Dubai, a city that has never failed to surprise me.

CHAPTER 44:
UNBALANCED SCALES

Surround yourself with people who make you happy. People who make you laugh, who help you when you're in need. People who genuinely care. They are the ones worth keeping in your life. Everyone else, including toxic family members, are just passing through —**Karl Marx**

* * *

Throughout my life—and consequently, throughout this book—I've endeavored to stay positive, even when faced with disaster and disillusionment. My career has taken me all over the globe, exposing me to a wide variety of different cultures and bringing me face-to-face with innumerable fascinating, unique people, many of whom I regret not getting to know better than I did. So I speak from a position of authority when I say that the majority of people, deep down, mean well, and are essentially decent. I've been on the receiving end of countless acts of kindness, without which I would have never made it to where I am today. Forget Dubai—I doubt I would have ever made it out of Manchester were it not for all the acts of decency from which I benefited, beginning with those carried out by my parents. Most of the strife I've experienced has come not from individual people but from undesirable circumstances or simply fate. I have a highly positive view, on the whole, of the human race, and virtually every time I interact with a fan, a colleague, or a fellow traveler, that impression of humankind is reconfirmed. For my part, I have tried to bring optimism and generosity into all of my dealings and to extend the benefit of the doubt to anyone I should happen to meet, even if I suspect they may not be doing me the same courtesy. Those encounters are comparatively rare but not unheard of. I can count on the fingers of one hand the people in my life who have challenged my sunny assessment of humanity –the people who have actively sought to impede me and frustrate my attempts to do what's right.

Families are complex structures that fall quickly into disrepair if they're not properly maintained. Even a superficially happy and seemingly intact family might be crumbling on the inside, developing hidden fractures and breaking into jutting jagged pieces. Family members owe it to one another to try and patch up those broken bits—or, if all else fails, to not deliberately exacerbate the issues and hasten the deterioration. I'd learned all about this, thanks to the breakdown of my parents' marriage, before I ever met Anne or the rest of the Riley clan, most of whom are lovely, dependable people. It seems to me, however, that there are a minority of human beings who are at their happiest and most in their element, not when things are placid, but when they are in turmoil. One such person is Anne's sister, who will go unnamed, and who has, in my eyes, regularly striven to sow division and sabotage attempts at peacemaking. All the jagged pieces seemed to get sharper and jaggeder when she was around. Her actions, driven by motives that only she can fully understand, have consistently been destructive and spiteful. Like any family, the Rileys have known periods of grief and loss. Such junctures, as painful as they are, can be positive things insofar as they offer family members a chance to come together and heal as a unit. Anne's sister, I am certain, is attracted, in a perverse way, to these unhappy periods. She sees them not as an opportunity to mend fences but rather a chance to divide and conquer. It's quite a sick mentality. She's never passed up the opportunity to escalate a low-stakes sibling squabble into a full-blown feud. It's almost impressive, in a twisted sort of way. She has a talent for negativity that's unmatched by anyone else I've ever met.

As I've tried to make clear, however, she is very much the exception that proves the rule. The overwhelming majority do not operate the way that she does. Even within the Rileys, she's an outlier. I don't want this to sound like a broadside at Anne's people or a generic screed about irritating in-laws, because I love the Rileys, on the whole, and it's been an honor to be counted among their number. Everyone in that family was born with a backbone of steel and a fierce sense of loyalty, traits they inherited from Bill and Fran, Anne's parents. The two of them, when they were alive, were a sort of lighthouse beacon for the other Rileys, guiding them through life's trials with grace and unwavering support. They were the heart and the soul of that family and its fearless helmsmen. For me, getting on well with them was always a breeze. Anne's brother Ste, too, is one of my oldest and closest friends. He and I have had the occasional falling out, but he's like a brother to me now. When I first met him, things between us got off to a rocky start, to put it mildly. He was only nine years old, a pint-sized young boy and Liverpool FC fanatic, still hanging onto memories of Anne's ex, and utterly unimpressed with this new guy, this Manchester United fan she'd brought home to meet everyone. As you can imagine, he didn't exactly give me a warm welcome. There was something almost comical about how far I bent over backward to get on that surly kid's good side--as if by winning him over, I could prove myself to all of his kin as well. Not my most dignified moment. But apparently, my charm offensive paid off in the long run, if our friendship as adults is anything to go on. My relationship with Ste's family is just brilliant. He and his wife, Mel (who we also love dearly) have 4 children – our nephews and nieces, Jamie, Hayley, Abbie and Lewis. It makes me so happy to be able to say just how close we are to all of them. We share vacations together, laugh together – cry together – I could not love them any more than I already do.

When Bill and Fran passed away, the Rileys were left adrift and rudderless. Their absence left a gaping hole that nothing and nobody could fill--a hole that Anne's sister exploited and actively made worse until it was wide and deep enough to damn near swallow the entire family. Without Bill and Fran's example to guide them, they were no longer anchored in civility and goodness, and things quickly got ugly. It makes me angry to think back on it, and I'm sure that anger is coming through. I did not want to leave it out of my life story or diminish it, as I think that would be wrong. I'm not looking to make enemies, but nor am I willing to wallpaper over the rough patches in my life and pretend they never happened. Anne and I are no longer in touch with that sister or with a few other Rileys who sided with her--I still resent that there had to be sides at all, but it was she who drew those battle lines. The kicker here is that in her quest to play the villain, she unwittingly did us a favor. Cutting off that constant source of drama and tension brought those of us who remained when the dust settled, closer together. Sure, the family gatherings have shrunk a bit, but the ones who stuck around are tighter than ever. Losing the old family dynamic was tough, no doubt about it. But that was the tradeoff that had to be made in order to have a life free from toxicity.

In a roundabout way, we all ended up finding our own kind of peace…and I am positive that Bill and Fran would have been okay with that. I don't want to pathologize her any more than I already have, but it's my belief that people like that, people who thrive on discord and misery, have to be spurred to behave the way they do by some deep-seated internal discontent that they cannot bring themselves to work through in a healthy way. That was my take on Jim Fontaine and his alcoholism and

200

my take on Ann and Phil's parents and their mooching. We all feel most comfortable, I think, as human beings, when our environment is a reflection of what we feel on the inside—and sadly, for some people, that means externalizing a lot of negative, damaging emotions.

* * *

The loss of a parent is a profound and life-altering event, one that brings a mix of sorrow, reflection, and an unexpected shift in family dynamics. When my Mum passed away, it was a devastating blow to all of us. My brothers and sisters and I tried our best to stick together, although there were inevitably some disagreements along the way. Wendy, my first "baby" sister, and I often found ourselves on opposite sides when it came to matters concerning our Mum. Our differing perspectives led to many heated arguments, each fueled by our own grief and individual experiences with her. But over time, we found a way to put our differences aside. We allowed our love for each other to take precedence, letting it guide us through the difficult process of healing. The bond we share today, despite our past conflicts, is a testament to the love we have for each other.

However, when my Dad passed away, the dynamics within our family took a darker turn. Unlike with my Mum, the unity we had managed to maintain began to unravel. My Dad had not done much to foster a strong, healthy relationship with the younger ones—especially Andrew and Peter. As a result, their feelings towards him were markedly different from mine. While I cherished the relationship I had with my Dad, they harbored unresolved resentment and indifference and I was completely unaware that the hurt went so deep. It was clear that Andrew and Peter, in particular, did not share my deep sense of loss. They knew how much I loved and respected our Dad, and it was during his death that they chose to express their feelings in the most hurtful ways imaginable.

Their sense of humor had always been somewhat twisted, but the things they said and did to me during that time crossed the line on so many levels. In their minds, it seemed that by hurting me, they were somehow exacting a form of revenge on our father, even in death. The ridicule and the cruel jabs were relentless, adding layers of pain to an already unbearable situation. To this day, I still grapple with understanding why they felt the need to lash out at me during such a vulnerable moment. Their actions left scars that are slow to heal, and the memory of their words still stings.

Navigating these complex and painful family relationships has been one of the most challenging aspects of my life. The loss of my parents not only brought grief but also revealed the deep-seated tensions and unresolved conflicts among us. Yet, through it all, I work hard to remember the good times, the love, and the shared memories that bind us together.

It's important to me that this chapter be an outlier in this book, the same way that Anne's sister is an outlier within the extended Riley family. I want this book to accurately reflect the shape and tenor of the life I've lived––and over the course of my life, the kindness I've seen has outweighed the cruelty to an incalculable degree. The scales, I'm happy to say, are nowhere near balanced.

CHAPTER 45:
NICK AND JULIA

The love of a family is life's greatest blessing.
*Today, we gain a daughter to share in that love —***Unknown**

* * *

When Anne hatched the idea for ABBAFab, it seemed to both of us like a modest solution to a temporary--and likely insoluble--problem. I wonder how she would have responded if I had been able to peer into our future, in that moment, and tell her all the extraordinary doors that it would open for us and all the happiness that it would make possible. I suspect she would have rolled her eyes at me and accused me of being weird, the same way she did when I told her that we would get married someday. That remains the only time in my life that I've evinced any oracular gifts. I could never have foreseen all the good that ABBAFab would do for us. Forestalling the closure of SKYE was, in the final estimation, the least of the strange miracles that it worked in our lives.

One of our ABBAFab tours, years after SKYE's closure, took us to the Rampart Casino in Las Vegas. That gig wound up being more fateful, more consequential, than perhaps any other we have ever played. It was our custom when we arrived at a venue and saw the stage for the first time, to nominate one of the band members to hop off-stage and make our introductions to the sound engineer. This particular night at the Rampart Casino, the sound engineer happened to be a woman in her early twenties named Julia. Nick took it upon himself to go over to the sound booth and introduce her to the band. His motivation wasn't difficult for the rest of us to figure out--I can easily picture myself volunteering that same way at that age. Julia's booth was about two-thirds of the way across the room, but even from my vantage point onstage, I could see that she and my son were getting on famously. They exchanged phone numbers and Facebook profiles that same night, and the rest, as they say, is history.

Two or three weeks later, Nick came to Anne and me with an unmistakable air of excitement about him that he was trying and failing to conceal. "Hey," he said,

"I'm headed to Vegas, I've got plans. Nothing romantic or anything. Just meeting someone in Vegas."

"Oh really. Who might that be?"

"Just that girl we met at the show. Julia. Not a date. Just visiting."

It was fated to be much more than a friendly visit--and much more than a casual date, for that matter. The two of them caught a Smashmouth concert in Vegas and had a great time, by all accounts. From then on, it was official. They started dating and never looked back. Before we knew it, they'd become all but inseparable. Julia is quite a forceful personality, in all the best ways, as we soon came to discover. She's from Canada and boasts a range of eclectic talents. In addition to her sound engineering work, she plays bass guitar and bassoon; she's a licensed forklift operator, a singer, and a dancer. Unsurprisingly, I was most intrigued by her musical and artistic talents. Given her diverse array of different aptitudes, it strikes me as even more of a stroke of luck that we met her when and where we did. She easily might have been busy plying another trade the night we played the Rampart Casino. But she wasn't.

Three or four years later, the bond between them had only deepened, and Nick confided in us that he was planning to propose. Julia is a massive *Lord of the Rings* fan. Nick, Anne, and I had a trip to Australia and New Zealand planned, and this presented an opportunity that my son knew he could not afford to pass up. We found our way to Hobbiton, a bucolic movie set left standing and converted into a tourist destination after production wrapped on the Peter Jackson films. I saw Nick and Julia wandering about with stars in their eyes. Nick can't quite match Julia's *Lord of the Rings* fanaticism, but he's a general fanatic for movies and pop culture--and he was starry-eyed for another reason, as Anne and I well knew. The two of us held back as he led Julia to the top of the hill outside Bilbo Baggins' hobbit hole, where he got down on one knee and proposed to her. It could not have been more idyllic. We made certain to call Wendy and Paul, Julia's parents on a video call and the four of us, together, watched the proposal and the subsequent acceptance. We were delighted to be there that day with both of them.

The onset of the pandemic interfered with their nuptials for the better part of two years, but they waited patiently, and when normalcy started to be restored, they made arrangements to be wed at the Rampart Casino in Vegas--the place where they'd first met. The reception was held in the very same room that ABBAFab had once played, the night she'd been in the sound booth. As you entered the room, your eyes fell upon a large circular carpet on the floor, about a third of the way out from the wall furthest from the stage, with a big X on it, to denote the exact spot where they had been standing, when Nick had introduced himself to her. That's one lovely little detail that will always stick with me.

Two separate crises arose that threatened to put a damper on things the weekend of the wedding. The first was beyond anyone's control. The second was the person that Nick selected to be his best man. He was a man who was considerably older than Nick, a man Nick had affectionately called "uncle" all through his childhood, a man that I once considered my best friend--and a man who has been entirely absent from this narrative up till now, owing to a falling out that he and I had, on the eve of Nick's wedding. There's a myriad of stories that I could tell about our 30-year friendship, most of them happy--and all of them, regrettably, tainted in hindsight by the way things ended between us. He and I were quite close, suffice to say. When Anne got pregnant with Nick, he shared in our elation. He was one of the first people to meet Nick at the hospital the morning he was born. Our families were once so close. We once drove straight through the night, with Nick slumbering in the backseat, after a gig in Blackpool that had ended at midnight, to attend the christening of their firstborn daughter--a feat that we were only able to accomplish, I think, because it happened to be the same night that Princess Diana died. The news reports, which started out upsetting and grew more and more shocking and tragic as the night wore on, were the only reason we managed to stay awake. "Oh, that's terrible," I can remember Anne saying before it became clear to us that Diana had been killed. "They're already talking about her in the past tense--like she's dead."

All of this is to say that I put a lot of stock in this man's friendship - our families were intertwined, and I anticipated decades of continued closeness and conviviality between us. That all ended the night before Nick and Julia were wed. Nick had hand-picked him to be his best man, in spite of the generational divide, because he had grown up admiring him and aspiring to be like him. Anne and I thought he was an unconventional choice, but we weren't about to supersede Nick when it came to his own wedding. He told us that it felt right, and that was good enough for us. Of course, having since seen how abominably Nick's one-time honorary uncle behaved during one of the most important events of his life, I do wish I'd stepped in and been a bit more adamant. He did none of the things that a best man is typically called upon to do, short of delivering an insincere, perfunctory speech. Of course, bearing in mind the once-in-a-lifetime event for which we were all together, any grievances he had could have - and should have, waited until after the wedding. But no ~ instead, he calls me on the evening before the wedding – a conversation that culminated in a scorched earth confrontation between him and myself in which he laid into me and railed against every last facet of the ceremony in which he had been called upon to (and agreed to) play a key, positive role. It was a despicable tirade that would have been galling and inappropriate coming from any of our guests, let alone one of my closest friends. Nick himself was not privy to any of this unpleasantness while it was unfolding--I made sure of that. I won't hide the fact that the breakdown of this friendship has hurt me more than any other. I still don't understand where it came from, but I do wish I could go back in time and change that one aspect on one of the happiest days of my life

Unfortunately, there was nothing I could do to protect Nick or Julia from the second, unrelated disaster that reared its ugly head the following day.

Julia was feeling a bit under the weather the morning of the wedding. We all wrote it off as dehydration or nerves. Perhaps we were too quick to do so, but we all earnestly wanted to keep the festivities running smoothly--and Julia herself, for what it's worth, was dead set on powering through it. That's just the sort of person she is--tenacious and not easily cowed, even when she's not feeling her best. Her mystery ailment steadily outpaced her ability to maintain a brave face, however. Midway through the wedding reception, during somebody's speech --I can't remember whose--she had to spring from her seat and race out of the room with all of her bridesmaids trailing behind her. As it turns out, she had come down with norovirus. Most of the guests didn't get another glimpse of her after that. She was violently sick and bedridden the rest of the day and couldn't partake in the rest of the wedding. She had gotten to dance with Nick before succumbing to the nausea but hadn't had the chance to do the father-daughter dance, which was a damned shame. Last year, we all traveled to Cyprus for the wedding of Nick's cousin Jamie, my nephew, and a few of us seized the chance to surprise Julia and her dad with a belated father-daughter dance, complete with the song that they had originally selected for her wedding. It satisfied me immensely to watch the two of them finally achieve closure, with no debilitating viruses--or disagreeable best men--anywhere in sight.

CHAPTER 46:
POLAR OPPOSITES

Family is not an important thing. It's everything
—Michael J. Fox

* * *

Taken as a whole, Nick and Julia's wedding was a wonderful occasion. Uncle Harry insisted on attending, for one thing, which was a joy to behold. I had been at his house perhaps four months prior. He hadn't been faring all that well, in terms of his health. His mobility had been reduced to the point that he was confined to a wheelchair. I started talking to him about the wedding, and he proclaimed, rather assertively for a man in his condition, "I want to go." My auntie and cousin laughed at him. "How can you go to the wedding? You can barely make it to the corner shop." He just kept repeating himself, his tone friendly but insistent, his eyes alight. "I want to go. I want to go to that wedding!" I could see that he wasn't about to back down--and frankly, I didn't want him to. "Alright," I said to him. "If you want to go, if you think you can make it on a plane, I'll buy you a ticket today." And that's what happened. He was in a wheelchair the whole time, but anyone who was there would tell you that he was the life and soul of the party, nearly upstaging the bride and groom.

We booked The Lords of 52nd Street, Billy Joel's original band, to perform for our assembled guests, the night before the wedding. Nick's a big fan of theirs, and we can all now confirm that they haven't lost their touch. You could still feel the electricity that had energized all those great hit singles of the 1970s and early 1980s. Everyone, including Richie Cannata, Liberty DeVito, Russel Javors – all original members of the Billy Joel Band – along with the rest of "The Lords", treated it like a big rock concert, and we all had a total blast. Several of us got the opportunity to hop onstage and perform with them, including Nick and myself. I know that was a dream come true for Nick in particular. Certain aspects of the wedding might have gone haywire, but that's rock and roll for you. Nick got through it all with the aid of his usual rock star swagger and panache. That's all you can do, when things don't quite go according to plan. He also wrote his own wedding song a gorgeous, heartfelt song for him and Julia called "They Call This Dance The First".

Julia is, in her own right, no less of a rock star. We couldn't wish for anyone better for Nick. They're perfect together, in spite of--or perhaps because of--all the ways in which they're unalike. In many respects, they're opposites. But she's a fantastic person, and together they make a fantastic couple. For what it's worth, Anne and I also get on very well with her. If your bond with your spouse is strong enough, passionate enough, then hitting it off with your in-laws is strictly optional--but it's a pleasant luxury, even still. One that ought not be taken for granted. Julia's become an important part of TAD Management, in the years since she and Nick first crossed paths. She's now one of the key players in ABBAFab, having basically taken over Anne's role after she retired. I've written before of the "TAD family," and I hope I've made it clear by now that that's not merely a figure of speech--it truly is a family affair, and I wouldn't have it any other way. It would have been enough--more than enough--if Julia had only made my son a happy man. But she's made all of our lives better, happier and fuller. The story of their love affair, from that first chance encounter in Vegas onward, has been a great turn of events for everyone who knows and loves either of them.

And our good fortune in Nick finding Julia doesn't end there. If there's anything more improbable than two newlyweds getting along with each others' parents, it's both sets of in-laws getting along just as well. Incredibly, that's the case with our two families. Not long ago, Anne and Nick and Julia and I, together with Julia's parents, took a trip to Antarctica, with a three-day stopover in Buenos Aires. There aren't all that many people I've known in my life that I would have rather ventured to the ends of the earth with. It was a highly unusual situation to find myself in--to realize that all four of us parents got along swimmingly, even without our kids around. Generally, you expect the kids to provide the social adhesive on getaways like that, and things start to come asunder when they're not around. But Nick and Julia could always take off and do their own thing and not have to worry about awkwardness or infighting setting in while their backs were turned. The four of us come from different walks of life, but none of that seems to matter when we're just hanging out. It was a wonderful vacation, one that underscored for me just how much luck factors into our happiness in this life. Seeing Antarctica's frozen majesty--and getting tipsy on

Argentinian wine––with Julia's parents, even helped to put the wedding's relatively insignificant hiccups into perspective for me.

I'm so thankful that Nick has many years of peaceable, stress-free family gatherings to look forward to. The fractiousness in Anne's family caused so much needless heartache for her and I. Nick and Julia don't need that sort of turmoil in their lives––nobody does. Even if you don't exactly see eye to eye on every issue with your family members, it's better to embrace your commonalities and try to celebrate your differences than to push people away and nurture your petty grievances until they've blossomed into deep hatred. You have to pick your enemies as carefully as you do your friends, reserving your scorn for the people in your life who have really wronged you. Writing this book would have been so much more draining and depressing if I'd had to re-litigate a different resentment in every other chapter. I've lived my life in such a way that it's been a pleasure to chronicle it because I've made friends everywhere I've gone, often in out-of-the-way places and under unusual and unpredictable circumstances. It wasn't difficult to live my life in this manner––quite the opposite, in fact. The more friends––and the fewer enemies––you have, the easier your life becomes.

I have to stress, however, that I still would have happily intertwined my life with Anne's even if she had been raised by wolves or born in a pit of vipers. She means that much to me. I've enjoyed many spectacular friendships, but none of them have pried open the deepest recesses of my heart the way that her companionship has. There's one more wedding that I must now recount, one that occurred about 20 years before Nick and Julia's, one that I've been saving until near the end of this book––my own. I've plucked it from its appropriate place on the timeline and sneaked it into this book's final pages because it serves as a summation of all the warmth, devotion and tenderness I've harbored for Anne Riley.

CHAPTER 47:
OUR HAPPILY EVER AFTER

Happily ever after is not a fairy tale. It's a choice
—**Fawn Weaver**

* * *

The love that I share with Anne is unspeakably profound and eternally lasting. It has come to define me more than anything else in my life and provided me with a role to play that has brought me more joy than any other, with the sole exception of father-hood. And even that part of my life has been made immeasurably sweeter thanks to Anne. The boundless love that I feel for her has flowed like tributaries into my love for Nick, and my love for music, and my love for travel. We raised our son together, we wrote and performed songs together, we saw the world together.

All of my passions, large and small, are inflected by her, and originate, in some way, in the great passion that she and I share. She has been my best friend, my best business partner, and the great romance of my life. She is, in short, everything to me. And so it might surprise you to learn that, despite having been together for decades, she and I did not actually get married until after we had already been together for 20 years – we were married on August 6th, 2003. Mark that down as the day that Anne Riley and I officially tied the knot, setting in stone, forever and always, what we both understood to be true––what we both knew was meant to be.

The road to that day was a wild ride. But you already know that. You've read all about it. The story of my path to the marriage altar is the story of my life in its totality, the story I've been telling you from page one––and Anne has been at my side for almost all of it. You would think, after all that, that getting hitched would be something of a formality, a footnote, an afterthought. Nothing could possibly be further from the truth. It was not a perfunctory addendum to our love affair, but rather its supreme culmination. And it was not without pitfalls. I can't even begin to tell you about all of the bureaucratic hoops that we had to jump through with regard to our immigration status, to make it all legally viable––not only because you'd be bored to tears if I did, but also because I didn't understand them all even as I was jumping through them. The labyrinthine bureaucracy we had to navigate, when we decided to get the law involved, was just as much of a pain in the ass as we'd always known it would be. In all honesty, that had probably been the main obstacle for Anne and me, all along. The number one thing that made it take so damn long. The longer we waited, the sillier it started to seem. After all, what could a marriage certificate possibly prove that we had not already proved to one another a thousand times over?

Well, let me put it this way: our union is worth considerably more than the paper it's printed on. Our belated wedding shaped up to be something of a gigantic, jubilant family campout. Our loved ones flew in from all corners of the UK and the US, transforming our home into a bustling hub of activity that exuded a palpable sense of warmth. Never in my life had I felt so much fondness consolidated under a single roof. In fact, our roof was not expansive enough to encompass it all––we had people bunking down wherever they could find a spot, and a few even found themselves calling it a night out in the garden, under the stars. Jack Guier, our friend from Washington, who had just moved into the place behind our own, actually contemplated knocking down the concrete fence separating our properties so that our guests had more room to roam about and so that our festivities could spill out crazily and be gloriously unconstrained. Some of the wedding attendees even wound up crashing at his place, which had the effect of turning the whole affair into a true community event. That was quintessential Jack.

Successive layers of love had been piling up between Anne and me for ages by the time we sealed the deal. It was a cumulative thing, and the atmosphere of our wedding reflected that. Our relationship was an institution in the lives of all who knew us. Everyone who attended our wedding knew precisely who we were and how good we were for each other. We had loved each other for so long that saying our vows felt less like we were pledging to spend the rest of our lives together--which clearly went without saying—and more like we were rejoicing in the wonderful joint life we'd already lived. It was not anticipatory but celebratory—and the celebration was richly deserved. Sometimes, even now, I catch myself reflecting on how out of my league that woman is. I've learned so much from her—more than I could ever convey via the written word. She's a wonderful woman, an awe-inspiring mother to Nick, and a ceaseless fount of wisdom and goodwill.

The morning of the wedding I was overcome with a level of nervous jitters that, I have to say, hardly befitted a man who was about to marry the woman he had already spent a huge portion of his adult life with. Anne and I ought to have been old pros after all we'd been through together. But how else am I to account for the fact that I don't remember so many of the little details of that incredible day, the sorts of things that would have stood out to a person less addled and giddy with excitement than myself? The takeaway from all this is simple: I was not going to take Anne Riley for granted. Not for a moment, not even after untold years of stable commitment—not even on the day that we were finally going to be wed.

Something magical happened that day at Val Vista Estates. I found myself sitting at a piano with Nick and my dad, all three of us playing a tune together. 3 generations sat at the piano together for the first and only time. I couldn't tell you what song we played–I'm surprised I was able to play at all in the state I was in. Somebody snapped a photo of the piano keys, with our six hands dancing nimbly across them.

You may not be able to hear the music when you look at that picture, but you can most definitely feel the love and joy radiating out from its flat surface and its frozen subjects, suffusing the room you're standing in, transporting you back to that transient moment in time. That photograph is one of my most treasured possessions.

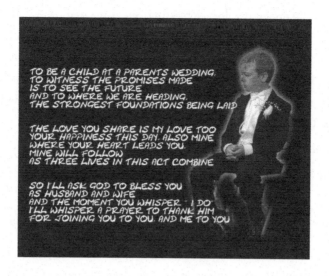

TO BE A CHILD AT A PARENTS WEDDING.
TO WITNESS THE PROMISES MADE
IS TO SEE THE FUTURE
AND TO WHERE WE ARE HEADING.
THE STRONGEST FOUNDATIONS BEING LAID

THE LOVE YOU SHARE IS MY LOVE TOO
YOUR HAPPINESS THIS DAY. ALSO MINE
WHERE YOUR HEART LEADS YOU.
MINE WILL FOLLOW
AS THREE LIVES IN THIS ACT COMBINE

SO I'LL ASK GOD TO BLESS YOU
AS HUSBAND AND WIFE
AND THE MOMENT YOU WHISPER I DO
I'LL WHISPER A PRAYER TO THANK HIM
FOR JOINING YOU TO YOU. AND ME TO YOU

Photos are not our only means of forcing time to stand still. When the limousine pulled up out front and Anne stepped out of it, the sight of her suspended time for me just as completely as any camera would have. There she was, looking more breathtakingly beautiful than I could have ever imagined. She just blew me away. I had been rendered speechless by her beauty on multiple continents, in all sorts of different circumstances, and at all hours of the day and night. She had been beautiful on interstates and out on the high seas when the wind had whipped at her hair. She had been beautiful on snowy slopes and on sandy beaches. She had been beautiful even when she was overtired or under the weather or just plain worn out from days of driving or flying or sailing. I had never known her to be anything other than beautiful--but I have never been more taken with her beauty than I was when she emerged from the back of that limousine.

The ceremony itself was a dream. We were surrounded on all sides by friends and family, encircled by the smiling faces of our loved ones. Nick recited a poem that tugged at everyone's heartstrings, a piece written by Anne and entitled "To Be a Child at a Parent's Wedding."

After that, our wedding song filled the air--Kenny Loggins' "For the First Time," a song that I can never listen to without crying. And when the tears flow, I once again feel that I'm standing at the altar with Anne, trembling all over, bathing in the radiance of her and of all those loving, familiar faces.

Having Anne in my life is a blessing. She is my best friend, my rock, my everything. She stood by me steadfastly when anyone in their right mind would have been tempted to walk away. There have been indiscretions, and they were all mine. I thank heaven that fate saw fit to bring us together in Torremolinos. My every action is guided by the wish to make her feel that everything we've endured together was worth it.

I told her once, in the lobby of a Spanish hotel, that I was going to marry her someday. On the one hand, this was a preposterous, unaccountable thing to blurt out. On the other hand, time has shown that it had the weight and substance of prophecy. Maybe I was channeling my future self at that moment. Maybe the Terry that had raised a child with her, married her and grown old with her was speaking to her across a gulf of time––making a promise to her that he knew he would one day honor, however glib and ridiculous it must have seemed to those two young people who had no idea what was awaiting them. Time has a way of melting like that for me when I think of Anne Riley and everything we've seen and shared. I cannot imagine a love stronger than what I feel for her.

We made it, Anne. This, right here, is our happily ever after.

CHAPTER 48:
LUCKY

When you have a close encounter with death and you survive,
there is a feeling of great gratitude
—T. D. Jakes

* * *

The Bus October 29th, 2023.

It was the usual, crazy, rockin' audience at the Coach House in San Juan Capistrano. The crowd was on fire, as always, and the Piano Men: Generations band was on fire with them! A good concert is a symbiotic thing, a feedback loop in which performers and listeners alike propel the energy levels higher and higher as the night progresses. And as satisfying as it is to knock one show out of the park, nothing can compare with stringing several successful shows together, one after another. It's like the high that athletes get when they're competing to the best of their ability and the high that gamblers get when they're on a hot streak, all rolled into one.

Without a doubt, the crowning jewel of my career has been performing alongside my incredibly talented son, Nick, in our sensational show, Piano Men: Generations. This show is far more than a tribute to the iconic music of Billy Joel and Elton John; it's a vibrant, dynamic experience that showcases the deep bond we share. Every note we play and every lyric we sing, reflects the humor, love, and mutual respect that defines our relationship.

From the moment the lights dim and the first notes are played, there's an electric anticipation in the air. Our performances are a symphony of emotion and energy, bringing the timeless music of Billy and Elton to life with a fresh, contemporary twist. The camaraderie between Nick and me is evident on stage, and it's this genuine connection that resonates with our audiences, creating an atmosphere that is both intimate and exhilarating.

Touring with a phenomenal band that features Chad Cole on Bass Guitar, Christian Phillips and Billy Tegethoff on guitars, Chris Whiteley on Sax and Keyboards and simply the best drummer I have worked with, Mike Richau, we have the privilege of performing in sold-out venues across the globe – traveling from city to city and sharing these unforgettable moments with Nick. It has not only been the highlight of my career but also the highlight of my life.

After the show at The Coach House, we packed up and hit the road to Palm Springs for another gig at the Oasis Club. Once we wrapped up there, we hopped back on the bus for the trip back to Arizona, a nice, short 4-and-a-half-hour drive.

Those two shows would have been as good a note as any to go out on––not that we had any intention of hanging up our spurs anytime soon. We still had far too much enthusiasm for our work and for all those wonderful crowds. But fate very nearly saw to it that we never played another show again––and never saw another sunrise.

I settled into my bunk ready to sleep on the way home, like I always do on these nighttime drives. Sleep came easy to me, so it didn't take long before I was out. I've taken enough tour buses and flights all over creation by now that sleep comes easily to me most nights, no matter where I lay my head, even when I'm zipping along at 70 miles per hour. Around 3:00 in the morning, however, I suddenly awoke, feeling surprisingly well-rested, considering what a hectic few days we'd had. Rather than tossing and turning and waiting for the sun to come up over the highway, I decided to head to the back of the bus, where I could check my emails and get my day started. Everyone else––Nick, Mike, Chad, Christian, Billy, and Chris––were all out cold in their bunks. Kael, our amazing driver, and I were the only ones who were awake.

I'll never forget that moment on the bus – the first hint of something not quite right as it swayed in a way that felt all too unfamiliar. It was just a subtle shift to the left, then to the right. Not a violent swerve, merely a seemingly unmotivated shift to the left, followed by an equally sudden shift to the right. It all transpired in the space of five or so seconds, and yet I could describe every detail of those scant few seconds as though they had lasted hours. They felt to me, in the moment, like an eternity, and that is how I remember them when I replay them in my mind. I can't shake off the fear that gripped me.

The movement grew more pronounced, the bus veering sharply to the left. And then came the noise – a bone-chilling, deafening roar - a heart-stopping sound that seemed to pierce straight through me. It didn't last long, but it filled me with a dread unlike anything else I have known in my lifetime. After that, all hell broke loose.

An SUV barreling towards us at 85 miles per hour, going the wrong way on the freeway, careened into our path. The impact was cataclysmic, our bus colliding head-on with the speeding vehicle. We were going 70 mph, he was going 85. The crash felt inevitable, a horrifying collision of forces. The other driver didn't stand a chance.

The world faded swiftly to black. Darkness enveloped me. From that point on, it's all a blur. I don't have any concrete memories of the impact itself. Just the deafening noise. I don't remember anything else. It just went black. I think that's how it ends when it eventually does end. When it hits you, that's it. No more memories. Everything goes black, and then it's over. But it didn't end for me that night on the highway. Incredibly, it didn't end for any of us.

"Where's my Dad? I can't find my Dad!!"

Those were the first words I was cognizant of hearing as I clawed my way out of unconsciousness. I later discovered that I had been thrown from the back sofa of the bus, headfirst, and ended up about 12 feet away, in the passageway, hitting a door frame hard. My head took a serious hit on the right side, but at that moment, I knew nothing except for Nick's frantic voice echoing in my ears, searching for me. I tried to shout, but nothing came out.

After I successfully commanded my hand to reach out of the wreckage and mustered up a feeble plea for help, Nick and Chad were able to find me. "Pull my Dad up," Nick shouted as he and Chad shifted the wreckage aside and pulled me up onto my feet.

When my son and I locked eyes, I saw a look of horror contort his face. "Oh my god," he said. I asked him––or tried to ask him––what was wrong. "Your head," he moaned, "your head. There's blood everywhere." Without a second's hesitation, I asked him to take a photo of my head with his phone. What I saw when he held his phone screen up to my eyes was a 5-inch gash on my forehead, with a white patch of exposed skull peeking through it. I didn't feel any pain. Shock, I suppose, will do that to you. All that I could focus on was the pillow I was holding in my hands––it was sodden with blood, and somehow I couldn't bring myself to just let it drop.

The thought that entered my bloodied head at that moment was curiously pragmatic: *let's get things in order.* Chalk that one up to my managerial instincts taking over in the midst of a crisis if you like. "Nick," I said, "call your Mom right away. Let her know what's happened. She'll want to hear it from you. Tell her I'm fine. Chad, let's do a headcount. It's pitch black in here. Let's make sure everybody is ok. Who are we missing?" Then I heard Nick's voice once again in the background. After calling his Mom, he gave the phone to me, and I talked with Anne, allaying her fears, while Nick helped Chad check on everyone. "Where's Christian? Christian's gone ~ I can't find him!" There was a fearful panic in Nick's voice that I had never heard before. When Anne heard this through the phone connection, she dropped to her feet…surely not Christian? We can't lose Christian.

I will always feel eternally grateful that Kael, our driver that evening, was behind the wheel. His actions, through years of experience driving these 45-foot Prevost Tour busses, no doubt saved us from a worse fate. Kael emerged from the crash largely unscathed, incredibly. A split-second decision likely saved Chad's life–– he caught a glimpse of the oncoming SUV en route to the bathroom and instinctively dove back into his bunk. Billy, who had also woken up just prior to the crash, was in the front section on a sofa nursing a concussion after he was hurled head-first into the front panel. But every one of us came through in one piece, more or less. All of us lived to breathe in the cool night air and survey the grisly and bizarrely cinematic scene, with its jumbles of shattered glass and heaps of twisted metal that caught the flashing lights of the approaching emergency vehicles.

Christian Phillips is a phenomenal guitarist, vocalist, and simply a wonderful human being. I can count on 2 hands the people I love and admire musically in my life and Christian is one of them. As I said, Christian had made his way to the passenger seat at the front of the bus just about one minute before the collision. He did not have time to put his seat belt on – but it was NOT having his seat belt on that likely saved his life (not that I am suggesting we all now travel in a vehicle without a seat belt!). When the impact happened, Christian was thrown, like a rag doll, through the windshield. In a bus this size, those front windows are easily 6 feet tall and 10-12 feet wide. Christian somehow managed to grab hold of the metal center divider and hold on for dear life, with a mangled SUV below him and looking directly into Kael's eyes as the bus unceremoniously and gradually slowed down before barreling into the center divider. As the bus hit the wall in the middle of the freeway, Christian was thrown from the bus and down the freeway about 15 feet. Nobody saw this but Kael. And nobody knew this at the time. We later learned that Christian, no doubt filled with adrenaline and a sheer desire to make sure he has more time to spend with Cai and Josie, his 2 amazing children, managed to stand up and wind his way through bewildered drivers trying to avoid the wreckage, to the side of the freeway. When the first ambulances arrived, Christian was rushed to the hospital, where he spent the next 3 weeks recovering from his severe head wounds and body burns.

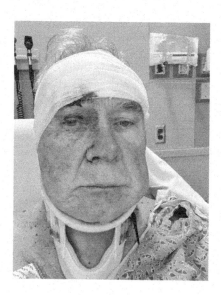

The rest of us were trapped inside the bus due to the damage the front of the bus had sustained in the collision. Within less than 20 minutes, the firefighters arrived to slice through the wreckage, providing a lifeline to safety with their fire ladders. Drew Baloh, a towering presence at 6'4", and a titan of the TAD family, somehow maneuvered his way past the hastily erected police barricades and made it to my side, just as the last of us were wriggling free of the wreck, with the aid of firefighters. Drew is also a talented performer regularly touring his tribute to Garth Brooks across the country. Drew is not someone you mess with. His no-frills personality and country grit were a tremendous aid to us that evening. Drew and I have a great relationship outside of TAD. He's a wonderful father to his 2 boys and a fantastic husband to his wife, Hana. He is one of the few crazy people I know who will jump on a plane for 48 hours just to watch Manchester United at Old Trafford - something we did together just last year! The severity of the situation was made real for me for perhaps the first time when I looked at Drew's face and saw fear etched upon it––fear that stood out all the more starkly punctuated as it was by the tears that glistened on his cheeks in the dim light and reaffirmed to me that somehow, we had cheated death that night.

Amidst the confusion, I recall Nick calmly guiding Anne on the route to the hospital. With Christian already rushed to medical care, we awaited our turn for transport to the hospital. The sun had started to rise which made the freeway scene all the more surreal and chaotic as we all boarded separate ambulances.

Yet, amidst the chaos, Nick traveled with me in the ambulance and his reassuring presence held fast as we clung to each other's hands throughout the journey. Seven hours stretched into eternity within the sterile confines of the hospital, a temporary home for most of the band.

The fact that we survived the crash at all feels nothing short of miraculous. Had we been in a smaller vehicle, I shudder to think of the outcome. The thought of Anne grappling with the loss of both Nick and myself is too much to bear. Recovery is a slow and arduous journey, both physically and mentally. Night driving and even being a passenger evoke a lingering unease - a reminder of the fragility of life. But despite the lingering scars, the Piano Men Generations band refuses to be sidelined. One by one we find ourselves reflecting on the miraculousness of our communal survival. We had all made it. Every last one of us.

CHAPTER 49:
FULL CIRCLE

Life is a wheel of fortune and it's my turn to spin it
—Tupac Shakur

* * *

That sort of violent brush with the great beyond is guaranteed to get you reflecting on things, and looking back over your life. Of course, that's the nature of this whole project––I was already mulling over this book, already in a nostalgic and ruminative state of mind, before I was hurled bodily onto the highway from the back of a moving bus. The crash was not the catalyst for all of these reminiscences––but it did crystallize certain things for me, and it reconfirmed the importance of the task that I've set for myself.

I am lucky that I have plenty of positive people in my life that I enjoy expending my energy on. Uncle Harry's widow and daughter, for example. I made good on the promise I made to him, just before he died.

Don't forget Barbara and Karen, he'd said. Well, I didn't.

Anne and I just hosted them at our place in Dubai a few weeks back. I read them a few work-in-progress passages from this book, pertaining to Harry––it must have taken me an hour to get through them, we were all crying so much. They brought some of his ashes with them, and we took the boat out into the bay and scattered them upon the water. I put on "MacArthur Park," and we hugged each other, and the tears flowed all over again. But it was anything but a sad occasion. The only sad outcome would have been if I had failed to honor Harry's deathbed request. It felt profoundly good, to do him proud one last time.

Anne and I divide our days roughly 50/50 between Arizona and Dubai, at this point in our lives. Arizona recently provided the backdrop for one of the many surprising and gratifying reunions that have occurred throughout my life at semi-regular intervals. Eric Johanson, the man who booked our first Red Lion gig after we got to America, recently moved to Arizona to enjoy his retirement, and he and I wound up reconnecting. He showed me a Polaroid of Anne and I that was taken the day that we auditioned for him. I was touched to learn that he had kept it all those years--and more touched still, when he insisted on giving it to us. "I could see right through you both, you know," he said. "You didn't have any gear. You told me you just hadn't brought it along, do you remember? I could tell you were bluffing. But I liked your sound, and I knew you were gonna be good." I had already known that we were hugely indebted to Eric, but I hadn't realized what an act of generosity and good faith he had bestowed upon us. We'd thought we had him fooled--but he had only ever been pretending to be fooled, for our sake.

I reached out to Ann and Phil recently, for the first time in many decades. Disparaging their parents, the way I do in this book's early chapters, wasn't sitting right with me--even if the parents deserved it--and I wanted to secure their blessing, and ask them if they wanted their names to be changed or in some way obfuscated. Ann's response was unexpectedly tender, candid, and eye-opening. *Quite honestly,* she wrote, *there is absolutely nothing you could say about my parents that I would be offended or distressed about.* She told me that her father passed away in 1983, and her mother followed suit in 1996. The two of them cast a long shadow over her life, and to hear her tell it, I had only ever seen a small portion of the terrors of which they were capable, just a brief glimpse of the dysfunction under which she and her brother had toiled. *My greatest sadness,* she told me, *is the way they were involved in other young peoples' lives, you being one of many.* Suddenly, I saw the whole Strawberry Pye chapter of my life in a new and more sinister light. I was not the last aspiring musician that they had exploited--and it was entirely possible that I hadn't even been the first.

I was dismayed to learn that the situation had been worse for Ann than I'd ever realized, but at the same time I was heartened by the openness with which she discussed that dark period, and by the readily evident fact that she had pulled through it and emerged intact. You don't have to survive a crash on the highway to know how it feels to narrowly evade being shredded to pieces. Life can devise all kinds of ways of smashing into you, and sending you reeling, and burying you in rubble. But Ann, like me, had clung to life amid the wreckage.

I sat back in my chair and thought about Strawberry Pye for a long time, after receiving her response--about how much that band had meant to all of us, back then, and about how far off those youthful priorities now seemed to me. It was a lifetime ago. But one of the privileges of being a musician is that it's relatively easy for us to turn back the clock--recording artists are always leaving records behind, time capsules of different epochs of their life.

After years of fruitless searching, I was finally able to track down an online listing for a physical copy of "Walkabout," the elusive song from my Strawberry Pye days, in a secondhand store in Amsterdam. I bought it and gave it a listen. It was definitely a recording of the times and it brought back so many wonderful memories of a time that helped to shape my life.

* * *

As I reflect on the incredible journey that has been my life, I cannot help but acknowledge the people who have played pivotal roles along the way. Among them are Jo and John Martin, whose partnership has profoundly impacted both my personal and professional life. In 2000, we embarked on a business venture with Jo Martin Management. Through thick and thin, including the challenging times brought by the pandemic, our collaboration has flourished. Jo manages 20-30 of the finest comedians and musical acts in the UK, and our synergy has only grown stronger.

But beyond the professional achievements, Jo and John have become much more than business partners. They are dear friends whose genuine warmth and integrity have enriched our lives in ways words cannot fully capture. Anne and I cherish the moments we spend with them, sharing laughter, stories, and a deep, trusting friendship that transcends the boundaries of work.

* * *

Around the year 2000, a business associate from Las Vegas, Ian Hammer, introduced me to a remarkable individual named Tim Flaherty. Tim, along with his wife Sonya, owns Entertainment Events Inc., a company with over three decades of experience in promoting shows. Ian suggested that Tim and I explore the possibility of working together, not knowing that Tim lived less than a mile from us!

Despite our different business styles, the synergy and mutual respect between Tim and me is beyond measure. This connection led us to form T2 Presents, a company that has been thriving and promoting shows worldwide. Our partnership in T2 Presents is just one facet of our relationship, which has blossomed both professionally and personally.

The four of us—Tim, Sonya, Anne, and I—share a fantastic rapport, enjoying the moments we get to spend together outside of business. The friendship and collaboration with Tim has significantly enriched my life over the past four years, bringing both joy and success. The journey with them has been nothing short of extraordinary, and I look forward to many more shared achievements and cherished memories.

* * *

Bob Conrad is one trusted colleague and friend with whom I've had the pleasure of working closely for over 20 years. Our journey together began at Skye, where Bob and I forged a strong professional bond that has stood the test of time.

Today, Bob continues to handle many of the concert promotions at TAD, and his credentials in the music industry are unparalleled. Having worked with legendary artists such as Billy Joel and Journey during their heyday, Bob's influence on the industry is undeniable. If a record was played on the radio back in the day, chances are it was Bob Conrad who made it happen.

Bob's expertise and dedication have been instrumental in the success of our ventures, and his contributions have left an indelible mark on the music industry. Beyond his professional achievements, Bob has been a steadfast and reliable partner, someone I can always count on....that is in addition to being, probably the "coolest" person on the planet!

CHAPTER 50:
A MIRACLE REVISITED

And in the end the love you take is equal to the love you make
—Paul McCartney

* * *

It's not easy for a musician to admit that his life's crowning achievement lies outside the realm of music. But in my case, there's no sense in denying it. If I were to never play another note, or sleep on another tour bus, or stand in another spotlight, I could still take solace in having my two supreme accomplishments by my side. My love for Anne, and the child that love produced, are the two great glories of my lifetime. I see so much promise in Nick, so much brilliance, so many beautiful qualities. If he ever writes a book like this one, I hope it makes mine look small and timid and tedious by comparison—-I want his adventures to dwarf mine, I want him to experience everything that life has to offer.

I've listened to a lot of the songs that meant the world to me when I was a teenager, as I've been penning these pages. Plenty of Wizzard, and Slade--and plenty of Gilbert O'Sullivan, too, which never fails to make Anne, Nick and Julia roll their eyes at me. They've always ribbed me for revering him the way I do. But there have been a few occasions when they've seen fit to adjourn their mockery, when the moment called for it. I was stunned, and reduced to floods of tears, when Nick and Julia bounded into the wedding reception to Gilbert O'Sullivan's song, Matrimony" just following the service and just before Julia was sick --a song they could have only picked in order to surprise me and cater to my tastes and my sentimental streak. A similar gesture from Nick once again got my waterworks going on Christmas in 2019 when he gifted me an envelope containing four tickets to see Gilbert O'Sullivan in LA. That show was canceled on account of the pandemic, but it was eventually rescheduled, and Nick and Julia came with me to see him perform. It was a small place, with a modest merchandise stall set up near the entrance. Two t-shirts, a coffee cup, some sheet music, and one or two other items. Nick asked me if I wanted a shirt or something, and I asked him to surprise me. Well, he certainly did--he bought me one of everything. I got to go backstage that day and meet Gilbert in his dressing room, which was simply extraordinary. More extraordinary still was the fact that I subsequently managed to book him for a performance at a venue that we own in Mesa. This was only four or five months ago. Getting to hang out with my lifelong hero in my own green room made my inner child indescribably giddy. It was as though I had actually gone on to play for Manchester United, the way I'd once fantasized about when I'd been kicking footballs around with my boyhood mates. Talking about life and music with Gilbert O'Sullivan, the guy I'd looked up to since I was 16, left me with a dazed, serene feeling. How many of us can say that we managed to achieve one of our loftiest and most infeasible adolescent dreams?

I bring this up not to applaud myself but to underscore, one final time, what a wonderful son I have in Nick, without whom I likely never would have met my musical idol--if there's anything I ought to be applauded for, it's raising that boy. He's shaping up to be a better man than me--and a truly top-shelf musician, at that. I recently had the privilege of witnessing his music come to life during a recording session with the Budapest Scoring Orchestra. He'd dedicated countless hours to arranging the majority of the 15 songs that he recorded with them, personally writing 13 of them, drawing inspiration from legends like John Williams, Alan Silvestri, and

Alan Menken. Seeing him transform, over the course of two days in Budapest, from a nervous and unsure songwriter to someone who confidently commanded the room made me indescribably happy and boundlessly proud. I personally heard world-class musicians whistling Nick's melodies as they made their way out of the recording studio after a 7-hour session. My heart burst with love for Nick at that moment, just as it had thirty years prior when I witnessed the miracle of his arrival into the world.

And speaking of miracles...

We've come to the end of the book, and there's only one more story that remains to be told. Structuring a book, arranging the chapters into the correct sequence, is very much like fine-tuning the order of songs in a set list. I knew before I wrote a single word of this memoir that the story I'm about to tell was the only one that could possibly supply the finale--the last song of the night.

My Little Miracle - Live

Around my 60th birthday, I found myself in Laughlin, Nevada, watching Nick perform in a casino with December '63 - a really stellar Franki Valli tribute band, of which he was a founding member. The concert was a perfect showcase for his comedy and audience engagement skills. I thought that nothing could make me happier than keeping my distance from the stage and watching him shine--but then he singled me out of the crowd, asked me to join him, and announced to the room that it was my 60th birthday. I obligingly got up onstage, expecting him to sing Happy Birthday to me or something along those lines. Instead, he began telling the audience the story of "My Little Miracle"--the song I wrote to commemorate his birth. I sat up there on that stage as he played a montage of photos of him and me, set to my song. I was overcome with emotion long before a slide came onscreen that read as follows:

But what he doesn't know... is that I wrote a response.

Nick had gone into the recording studio, unbeknownst to me, and recorded a new verse to cap off the song, a third verse that was in conversation with the verses I wrote when he was a baby.

MY LITTLE MIRACLE – RESPONSE

You say that I'm a miracle

And even if it's true

I wouldn't be this person

If it hadn't been for you

As years go by

And first impressions must be made by me

I'm hoping that my father

Is the man that they will see

There are moments that I've cherished

There are clothes that I've outgrown

And soon I'll be a grown-up

With a family of my own

But wherever life may take me

Wherever I may go

I'll always take you with me

Without Terry, there'd be no…

Nickolas…

* * *

A geyser of love surged up within me, as I sat there onstage, with his arm around my quivering shoulders. From that day on, "My Little Miracle" became a duet--a song that we performed together, as father and son. And this is how it always ends:

Nickolas...

[Terry] You're my pride and joy [Nick] I'm your baby boy

[Terry] My precious baby boy [Nick] How did I get

[Both] Everything I prayed for

Nickolas...

[Terry] All my dreams are different now [Nick] Dreams are different now

[Terry] You got to me somehow [Nick] And I'm proud that

[Terry] You're my miracle [Nick] I'm your miracle

[Terry] You're my

[Both] Little miracle

* * *

I want to conclude this book by noting once again, for posterity, just how incapable I am of expressing what Nickolas means to me and what a spectacular, happy,
generous, and compassionate person he is. All of those traits came to the forefront
when he took it upon himself to supplement my song--to make it the song that it
was always meant to be. In the same way that he helped that song achieve its potential, when no one else could have, he has completed his mother and I, and saturated
our lives with love, in a way that nothing else ever has, or ever will. Creating that
third verse is one of the most meaningful things that anyone has ever done for me.
If reading this book stirs his heart the way that hearing that new verse stirred mine,
then I will regard this whole thing as worthwhile, whatever else happens.

This book is for you, Nick. And for you, Anne.

Thank you for making it worth writing--thank you for making my life
worth living.

* * *

EPILOGUE:
IT'S BETTER TO FORGIVE...

One of the most important lessons I have learned in life is the power of forgiveness. It's easy to hold grudges and dwell on past hurts, but this only serves to weigh us down and prevent us from moving forward. It's far better to forgive than to forget, for in doing so, we free ourselves from the burden of resentment and anger.

So if there is anything I would wish for all of you, it would be to go forth with hope in your heart and a spirit of adventure in your soul. Believe in yourself, and remember that the biggest benefactor of forgiveness is the forgiver. Forgivers create a world filled with love, compassion, and forgiveness.

With much love,

Terry xx